M000227779

# chicken

## 100 **everyday** recipes

First published in 2011
LOVE FOOD is an imprint of Parragon Books Ltd

Parragon
Queen Street House
4 Queen Street
Bath BA1 1HE, UK

Copyright © Parragon Books Ltd 2011

LOVE FOOD and the accompanying heart device is a registered trade mark of Parragon Books Ltd in Australia, the UK, USA, India, and the EU

ISBN: 978-1-4454-3048-5

Printed in China

Produced by Ivy Contract
Photography by Charlie Paul

### Notes for the Reader

This book uses imperial, metric, or US cup measurements. Follow the same units of measurement throughout; do not mix imperial and metric. All spoon measurements are level: teaspoons are assumed to be 5 ml, and tablespoons are assumed to be 15 ml. Unless otherwise stated, milk is assumed to be full fat, eggs and individual vegetables are medium, and pepper is freshly ground black pepper.

The times given are an approximate guide only. Preparation times differ according to the techniques used by different people and the cooking times may also vary from those given. Optional ingredients, variations or serving suggestions have not been included in the calculations.

Recipes using raw or very lightly cooked eggs should be avoided by infants, the elderly, pregnant women, convalescents, and anyone suffering from an illness. Pregnant and breastfeeding women are advised to avoid eating peanuts and peanut products. Sufferers from nut allergies should be aware that some of the ready-made ingredients used in the recipes in this book may contain nuts. Always check the packaging before use. Vegetarians should be aware  that some of the ready-made ingredients used in the recipes in this book may contain animal products. Always check the packaging before use.

# chicken

# introduction

Chicken has become one of the most useful and popular meats in nearly all cultures around the world. The reasons for this are many, not least that chickens are relatively quick and easy to raise, and do not require acres of lush grassland! It is worth bearing in mind that a free-range, corn-fed chicken might cost a little more, but it will have a far superior flavor to one that has been intensively farmed.

From a nutritional point of view, chicken is an excellent source of protein, B vitamins, and minerals such as zinc and iron. It is naturally low in fat and has no carbohydrates, making it the dream food for those who need to keep their weight or cholesterol levels in check. It is very quick and easy to cook, too, so there need be no excuses about not having enough time to produce a healthy, well-balanced meal!

And from a gastronomic point of view? There are so many options that you could serve chicken every day of the week and still not run out of ideas! Chicken can be cooked very simply—roasted, chargrilled, broiled, stir-fried, or pan-fried—and served with potatoes or rice and salad greens or lightly cooked vegetables. And when you have a little more time to spare, the choices are endless. If you like rice, you can go for a creamy Italian risotto or a saffron-colored Spanish paella; and if you are a pasta lover, you will find some fantastic sauces. If Mexican food is your thing, there are traditional recipes to suit you; and there are Chinese, Thai, and Indian dishes to satisfy any spice cravings.

Whatever your choice, you will enjoy the flavor and variety these recipes have to offer.

# soups, starters & salads

# cream of chicken soup

## ingredients

### serves 4

3 tbsp butter

4 shallots, chopped

1 leek, sliced

1 lb/450 g skinless, boneless chicken breasts, chopped

1¾ pints/1 litre/2½ cups chicken stock

1 tbsp chopped fresh parsley

1 tbsp chopped fresh thyme, plus extra sprigs to garnish

¾ cup heavy cream

salt and pepper

## method

1 Melt the butter in a saucepan over medium heat. Add the shallots and cook, stirring, for 3 minutes, until softened. Add the leek and cook for another 5 minutes, stirring. Add the chicken, stock, parsley, and thyme and season. Bring to a boil, then simmer for 25 minutes, until the chicken is cooked through. Remove from the heat and let stand to cool for 10 minutes.

2 Transfer the soup to a food processor or blender and process until smooth (you may need to do this in batches). Return the soup to the rinsed-out pan and warm over low heat for 5 minutes.

3 Stir in the cream and cook for another 2 minutes, then remove from the heat and ladle into serving bowls. Garnish with sprigs of thyme and serve immediately.

## variation

For a low fat option, omit the heavy cream and replace half the chicken stock with low fat milk. The soup will still taste smooth and creamy.

# chicken & potato soup with bacon

## ingredients

### serves 4

1 tbsp butter
2 garlic cloves, chopped
1 onion, sliced
9 oz/250 g smoked, lean
     bacon, chopped
2 large leeks, sliced
2 tbsp all-purpose flour
1¼ pints/1 litre/4 cups
     chicken stock
1 lb 12 oz/800 g potatoes,
     chopped
7 oz/200 g skinless, boneless
     chicken breast, chopped
4 tbsp heavy cream
salt and pepper
broiled strips of bacon and sprigs
     of fresh flat-leaf parsley,
     to garnish

## method

1 Melt the butter in a large saucepan over medium heat. Add the garlic and onion and cook, stirring, for 3 minutes, until slightly softened. Add the chopped bacon and leeks and cook for another 3 minutes, stirring continuously.

2 In a bowl, mix the flour with enough stock to make a smooth paste, then stir it into the pan. Cook, stirring, for 2 minutes. Pour in the remaining stock, then add the potatoes and chicken. Season with salt and pepper. Bring to a boil, then lower the heat and simmer for 25 minutes, until the chicken and potatoes are tender and cooked through.

3 Stir in the cream and cook for another 2 minutes, then remove from the heat and ladle into serving bowls. Garnish with the broiled bacon and flat-leaf parsley, and serve immediately.

# chicken & broccoli soup

## ingredients

*serves 4–6*

8 oz/225 g head broccoli
2 oz/55 g unsalted butter
1 onion, chopped
8 oz/225 g/1⅓ cups basmati rice
8 oz/225 g skinless, boneless
    chicken breast, cut into
    thin slivers
1 oz/25 g/scant ¼ cup all-purpose
    whole wheat flour
10 fl oz/300 ml/1¼ cups milk
16 fl oz/500 ml/2 cups chicken
    stock
2 oz/55 g/generous ⅓ cup corn
    kernels
salt and pepper

## method

1 Break the broccoli into small florets and cook in a pan of lightly salted boiling water for 3 minutes, drain, then plunge into cold water and set aside.

2 Melt the butter in a pan over medium heat, add the onion, rice, and chicken, and cook for 5 minutes, stirring frequently.

3 Remove the pan from the heat and stir in the flour. Return to the heat and cook for 2 minutes, stirring constantly. Stir in the milk and then the stock. Bring to a boil, stirring continuously, then reduce the heat and let simmer for 10 minutes.

4 Drain the broccoli and add to the pan with the corn and salt and pepper. Let simmer for 5 minutes, or until the rice is tender, then serve.

# thai chicken-coconut soup

## ingredients

*serves 4*

4 oz/115 g dried vermicelli noodles

2 pints/1.2 litres/5 cups chicken
  or vegetable stock

1 lemongrass stalk, crushed

½-inch/1-cm piece fresh ginger,
  peeled and finely chopped

2 fresh kaffir lime leaves, thinly
  sliced

1 fresh red chile, or to taste,
  seeded and thinly sliced

2 skinless, boneless chicken
  breasts, thinly sliced

scant 1 cup coconut cream

2–3 tbsp Thai fish sauce

1–2 tbsp fresh lime juice

⅔ cup beansprouts

4 scallions, green part only,
  finely sliced

fresh cilantro leaves, to garnish

## method

*1* Soak the dried noodles in a large bowl with enough lukewarm water to cover for 20 minutes, until soft. Or, cook according to the package directions. Drain well and set aside.

*2* Meanwhile, bring the stock to a boil in a large pan over high heat. Lower the heat, add the lemongrass, ginger, lime leaves, and chile, and cook for 5 minutes. Add the chicken and continue simmering for another 3 minutes, or until cooked.

*3* Stir in the coconut cream, fish sauce, and 1 tablespoon of lime juice and continue simmering for 3 minutes. Add the beansprouts and scallions and simmer for another 1 minute.

*4* Taste and gradually add extra fish sauce or lime juice to the pan, if needed. Remove and discard the lemongrass stalk.

*5* Divide the vermicelli noodles among 4 bowls. Bring the soup back to a boil, then add to each bowl. The heat of the soup will warm the noodles. To garnish, sprinkle with cilantro leaves.

# chicken & tarragon soup

## ingredients

### serves 4

2 oz/55 g unsalted butter
1 large onion, chopped
10½ oz/300 g cooked skinless
    chicken, finely shredded
20 fl oz/625 ml/2½ cups
    chicken stock
1 tbsp chopped fresh tarragon
5 fl oz/150 ml/⅔ cup heavy cream
salt and pepper
fresh tarragon leaves, to garnish
deep-fried croutons, to serve

## method

1 Melt the butter in a large pan and fry the onion for
   3 minutes.

2 Add the chicken to the pan with half of the chicken
   stock. Bring to a boil, then reduce the heat and let
   simmer for 20 minutes. Let cool, then process until
   smooth in a blender or food processor.

3 Return the soup to the pan to heat through. Add the
   remainder of the stock, season with salt and pepper,
   and heat through. Add the chopped tarragon, then
   transfer the soup to individual serving bowls and stir
   in the cream.

4 Garnish the soup with fresh tarragon and serve with
   deep-fried croutons.

# clear soup with mushrooms & chicken

## ingredients

*serves 4*

1 oz/25 g/¼ cup dried porcini
    or other mushrooms
32 fl oz/1 liter/4 cups water
2 tbsp vegetable or peanut oil
4 oz/115 g mushrooms, sliced
2 garlic cloves, coarsely chopped
2-inch/5-cm piece fresh galangal,
    thinly sliced
2 chicken breast portions
    (on the bone, skin on)
8 oz/225 g baby cremini or white
    mushrooms, cut into fourths
juice of ½ lime
sprigs fresh flat-leaf parsley,
    to garnish

## method

1 Place the dried mushrooms in a small bowl and pour over hot water to cover. Set aside to soak for 20–30 minutes. Drain the mushrooms, reserving the soaking liquid. Cut off the stalks and chop the caps coarsely.

2 Pour the reserved soaking water into a pan with the water and bring to a boil. Reduce the heat to a simmer.

3 Meanwhile, heat the oil in a wok and stir-fry the soaked mushrooms, sliced fresh mushrooms, garlic, and galangal for 3–4 minutes. Add to the pan of hot water with the chicken breasts. Let simmer for 10–15 minutes, until the meat comes off the bones easily.

4 Remove the chicken from the pan. Peel off and set aside the skin. Remove the meat from the bones, slice, and set aside. Return the skin and bones to the stock and let simmer for an additional 30 minutes.

5 Remove the pan from the heat and strain the stock into a clean pan through a strainer lined with cheesecloth. Bring back to a boil and add the cremini or white mushrooms, sliced chicken, and lime juice. Reduce the heat and let simmer for 8-10 minutes. Ladle into warmed bowls, garnish with parsley sprigs, and serve immediately.

# chicken crostini

## ingredients

### serves 4

12 slices French bread
    or country bread
4 tbsp olive oil
2 garlic cloves, chopped
2 tbsp finely chopped fresh
    oregano
3½ oz/100 g cold roast chicken,
    cut into small, thin slices
4 tomatoes, sliced
12 thin slices of goat cheese
12 black olives, pitted and chopped
salt and pepper
fresh salad greens, to serve

## method

1 Put the bread under a preheated medium broiler and lightly toast on both sides. Meanwhile, pour the olive oil into a bowl and add the garlic and oregano. Season with salt and pepper and mix well. Remove the toasted bread slices from the broiler and brush them on one side only with the oil mixture.

2 Place the bread slices, oiled sides up, on a cookie sheet. Put some sliced chicken on top of each one, followed by a slice of tomato.

3 Divide the slices of goat cheese among the bread slices, then top with the chopped olives. Drizzle over the remaining oil mixture and transfer to a preheated oven, 350°F/180°C. Bake for about 5 minutes, or until the cheese is golden and starting to melt.

4 Remove from the oven and serve on a bed of fresh salad greens.

# chicken-noodle soup

## ingredients

### serves 4–6

2 skinless, boneless chicken breasts
3½ pints/2 liters/8 cups water
1 onion, with skin left on,
    cut in half
1 large garlic clove, cut in half
½-inch/1-cm piece fresh ginger,
    peeled and sliced
4 black peppercorns, lightly
    crushed
4 cloves
2 star anise
1 carrot, peeled
1 celery stalk, chopped
3½ oz/100 g baby corn, cut in half
    lengthwise and chopped
2 scallions, finely shredded
4 oz/115 g dried rice vermicelli
    noodles
salt and pepper

## method

1 Put the chicken breasts and water in a pan over high heat and bring to a boil. Lower the heat to its lowest setting and let simmer, skimming the surface until no more foam rises. Add the onion, garlic, ginger, peppercorns, cloves, star anise, and a pinch of salt and continue to simmer for 20 minutes, or until the chicken is tender and cooked through. Meanwhile, grate the carrot along its length on the coarse side of a grater so you get long, thin strips.

2 Strain the chicken, reserving about 2 pints/1.25 liters/ 5 cups stock, but discarding any flavoring ingredients. (At this point you can let the stock cool and refrigerate overnight, so any fat solidifies and can be lifted off and discarded.) Return the stock to the rinsed-out pan with the carrot, celery, baby corn, and scallions and bring to a boil. Boil until the baby corn are almost tender, then add the noodles and continue boiling for 2 minutes.

3 Meanwhile, chop the chicken, add it to the pan, and continue cooking for about 1 minute until the chicken is reheated and the noodles are soft. Add seasoning and serve in warmed bowls.

# crispy chicken & ham croquettes

## ingredients

*makes 8*

4 tbsp olive oil
4 tbsp all-purpose flour
7 fl oz/200 ml/scant 1 cup milk
4 oz/115 g cooked chicken, ground
2 oz/55 g serrano or cooked ham,
   very finely chopped
1 tbsp chopped fresh flat-leaf
   parsley, plus extra sprigs
   to garnish
small pinch of freshly
   grated nutmeg
1 egg, beaten
2 oz/55 g/1 cup day-old white
   bread crumbs
corn oil, for deep-frying
salt and pepper
garlic mayonnaise, to serve

## method

1 Heat the olive oil in a pan. Stir in the flour to form a paste and cook gently for 1 minute, stirring constantly. Gradually stir in the milk until smooth and slowly bring to a boil, stirring, until the mixture boils and thickens.

2 Remove from the heat, add the ground chicken, and beat until the mixture is smooth. Add the chopped ham, parsley, and nutmeg and mix well together. Season with salt and pepper. Put in a dish and let stand for 30 minutes, until cool, then cover and let rest in the refrigerator for 2–3 hours or overnight.

3 Pour the beaten egg onto a plate and spread out the bread crumbs on another plate. Divide the chilled chicken mixture into 8 portions, then shape to form cylindrical croquettes. Dip them, one at a time, in the beaten egg, then roll in the bread crumbs to coat. Let chill in the refrigerator for 1 hour.

4 Heat the oil in a deep-fryer to 350–375°F/180–190°C. Add the croquettes, in batches to prevent the temperature of the oil dropping, and deep-fry for 5–10 minutes, or until golden brown and crispy. Remove with a slotted spoon and drain well on paper towels.

5 Serve the croquettes piping hot, garnished with parsley sprigs, with garlic mayonnaise.

# chicken in lemon & garlic

## ingredients

### serves 6–8

4 large skinless, boneless
    chicken breasts
5 tbsp Spanish olive oil
1 onion, finely chopped
6 garlic cloves,
    finely chopped
grated rind of 1 lemon, finely pared
    zest of 1 lemon and juice of
    both lemons
4 tbsp chopped fresh flat-leaf
    parsley, plus extra to garnish
salt and pepper
lemon wedges and crusty bread,
    to serve

## method

1 Using a sharp knife, slice the chicken breasts widthwise
   into very thin slices. Heat the olive oil in a large,
   heavy-bottom skillet, add the onion and cook for
   5 minutes, or until softened, but not browned. Add
   the garlic and cook for an additional 30 seconds.

2 Add the sliced chicken to the skillet and cook gently
   for 5–10 minutes, stirring from time to time, until all
   the ingredients are lightly browned and the chicken
   is tender.

3 Add the grated lemon rind and the lemon juice and
   let it bubble. At the same time, deglaze the skillet by
   scraping and stirring all the bits on the bottom of the
   skillet into the juices with a wooden spoon. Remove
   the skillet from the heat, stir in the parsley, and season
   with salt and pepper.

4 Transfer, piping hot, to a warmed serving dish. Sprinkle
   with the pared lemon zest, garnish with the parsley,
   and serve with lemon wedges for squeezing over the
   chicken, accompanied by chunks or slices of crusty
   bread for mopping up the juices.

# soy chicken wings

## ingredients

### serves 3–4

9 oz/250 g chicken wings,
    defrosted if frozen
8 fl oz/250 ml/1 cup water
1 tbsp sliced scallion
1-inch/2.5-cm piece of fresh
    ginger, cut into 4 slices
2 tbsp light soy sauce
½ tsp dark soy sauce
1 star anise
1 tsp sugar

## method

1 Wash and dry the chicken wings. In a small pan, bring the water to a boil, then add the chicken, scallion, and fresh ginger and bring back to a boil.

2 Add the remaining ingredients, then cover and simmer for 30 minutes.

3 Using a slotted spoon, remove the chicken wings from any remaining liquid and serve hot.

# chicken liver pâté

## ingredients

### serves 6–8

6 oz/175 g unsalted butter

1 lb 2 oz/500 g chicken livers, thawed if frozen, and trimmed

½ tbsp sunflower oil

2 shallots, finely chopped

2 large garlic cloves, finely chopped

2½ tbsp Madeira or brandy

2 tbsp heavy cream

1 tsp dried thyme

¼ tsp ground allspice

salt and pepper

toasted slices brioche and mixed salad greens, to serve

## method

1 Melt 1 oz/30 g of the butter in a large skillet over medium-high heat. Add the chicken livers and stir for 5 minutes, or until they are brown on the outside, but still slightly pink in the centers. Work in batches, if necessary, to avoid overcrowding the pan.

2 Transfer the livers and their cooking juices to a food processor. Melt another 1 oz/30 g of the butter with the oil in the pan. Add the shallots and garlic and sauté, stirring frequently, for 2–3 minutes, until the shallots are soft, but not brown.

3 Add the Madeira and scrape up any cooking juices from the base. Stir in the cream, then the thyme, allspice, salt, and pepper. Pour this mixture, with the cooking juices, into the food processor with the livers. Add the remaining butter, cut into small pieces.

4 Whiz the mixture in the food processor until smooth. Taste, and adjust the seasoning if necessary. Let the mixture cool slightly, then scrape into a serving bowl and set aside to allow the pâté to cool completely.

5 Serve immediately, or cover the pâté and store in the refrigerator for up to 3 days and let stand at room temperature for 30 minutes before serving. Serve with hot toasted brioche and mixed salad greens.

# mixed greens with warm chicken livers

## ingredients

*serves 4*

9 oz/250 g mixed salad greens,
    torn into bite-size pieces
2 tbsp chopped fresh
    flat-leaf parsley
2 tbsp snipped fresh chives
3–4 tbsp olive oil
3½ oz/100 g shallots,
    finely chopped
1 large garlic clove,
    finely chopped
1 lb 2 oz/500 g chicken livers,
    cored, trimmed and halved
3 tbsp raspberry vinegar
salt and pepper
French bread, to serve (optional)

## method

1 Toss the salad greens with the parsley and chives and
   divide among individual plates.

2 Heat 2 tablespoons of the oil in a sauté pan or skillet
   over medium–high heat. Add the shallots and garlic
   and sauté for 2 minutes, or until the shallots are soft,
   but not brown.

3 Add an extra tablespoon of the oil to the sauté
   pan and heat. Add the chicken livers and sauté for
   5 minutes, or until they appear just pink in the center
   when cut in half. Add a little extra oil to the pan while
   the chicken livers are sautéeing, if necessary.

4 Increase the heat to high, then add the raspberry
   vinegar and stir quickly. Season with salt and pepper,
   then spoon the livers and cooking juices over the
   mixed greens. Serve immediately with French bread,
   if using.

# chicken, cheese & arugula salad

## ingredients

### serves 4

5½ oz/150 g arugula leaves
2 celery stalks, trimmed and sliced
½ cucumber, sliced
2 scallions, trimmed and sliced
2 tbsp chopped fresh parsley
1 oz/25 g walnut pieces
12 oz/350 g boneless roast
    chicken, sliced
4½ oz/125 g Stilton cheese, cubed
handful of seedless red grapes,
    cut in half (optional)
salt and pepper

### dressing

2 tbsp olive oil
1 tbsp sherry vinegar
1 tsp Dijon mustard
1 tbsp chopped mixed herbs

## method

1 Wash the arugula leaves, pat dry with paper towels, and put them into a large salad bowl. Add the celery, cucumber, scallions, parsley, and walnuts and mix together well. Transfer onto a large serving platter. Arrange the chicken slices over the salad, then scatter over the cheese. Add the red grapes, if using. Season well with salt and pepper.

2 To make the dressing, put all the ingredients into a screw-top jar and shake well. Alternatively, put them into a bowl and mix together well. Drizzle the dressing over the salad and serve.

# roast chicken salad with orange dressing

## ingredients

### serves 4

9 oz/250 g young spinach leaves
handful of fresh parsley leaves
½ cucumber, thinly sliced
3¼ oz/90 g/generous ¼ cup
    walnuts, toasted and chopped
12 oz/350 g boneless lean roast
    chicken, thinly sliced
2 red apples
1 tbsp lemon juice
fresh flat-leaf parsley sprigs,
    to garnish
orange wedges, to serve

### orange dressing

2 tbsp extra virgin olive oil
juice of 1 orange
finely grated rind of ½ orange
1 tbsp sour cream

## method

1 Wash and drain the spinach and parsley leaves, if
necessary, then arrange on a large serving platter. Top
with the cucumber and walnuts. Arrange the chicken
slices on top of the leaves.

2 Core the apples, then cut them in half. Cut each half
into slices and brush with the lemon juice to prevent
discoloration. Arrange the apple slices over the salad.

3 Place all the dressing ingredients in a screw-top jar,
screw on the lid tightly, and shake well until thoroughly
combined. Drizzle the dressing over the salad, garnish
with parsley sprigs, and serve immediately with
orange wedges.

# chicken pinwheels with blue cheese & herbs

## ingredients

### serves 4

2 tbsp pine nuts, lightly toasted

2 tbsp chopped fresh parsley

2 tbsp chopped fresh thyme

1 garlic clove, chopped

1 tbsp grated lemon rind

4 large, skinless, boneless chicken breasts

9 oz/250 g blue cheese, such as Stilton, crumbled

salt and pepper

twists of lemon and sprigs of fresh parsley, to garnish

fresh salad greens, to serve

## method

1 Put the pine nuts into a food processor with the parsley, thyme, garlic, and lemon rind. Season with salt and pepper.

2 Pound the chicken breasts lightly to flatten them. Spread them on one side with the pine nut mixture, then top with the cheese. Roll them up from one short end to the other, so that the filling is enclosed. Wrap the rolls individually in aluminum foil, and seal well. Transfer to a steamer, or a metal colander placed over a pan of boiling water, cover tightly, and steam for 10–12 minutes, or until cooked through.

3 Arrange the salad greens on a large serving platter. Remove the chicken from the heat, discard the foil, and cut the chicken rolls into slices. Arrange the slices over the salad greens, garnish with twists of lemon, and sprigs of parsley, and serve.

# cajun chicken salad

## ingredients

### serves 4

4 skinless, boneless chicken
    breasts, about 5 oz/140 g each
4 tsp Cajun seasoning
2 tsp corn oil (optional)
1 ripe mango, peeled, pitted, and
    cut into thick slices
7 oz/200 g mixed salad greens
1 red onion, thinly sliced and
    cut in half
6 oz/175 g cooked beet, diced
3 oz/85 g radishes, sliced
2 oz/55 g/scant ½ cup walnut
    halves
4 tbsp walnut oil
1–2 tsp Dijon mustard
1 tbsp lemon juice
2 tbsp sesame seeds
salt and pepper

## method

*1* Make 3 diagonal slashes across each chicken breast. Put the chicken into a shallow dish and sprinkle all over with the Cajun seasoning. Cover and let chill for at least 30 minutes.

*2* When ready to cook, brush a grill pan with the corn oil, if using. Heat over high heat until very hot and a few drops of water sprinkled into the pan sizzle immediately. Add the chicken and cook for 7–8 minutes on each side, or until thoroughly cooked. If still slightly pink in the center, cook a little longer. Remove the chicken and set aside.

*3* Add the mango slices to the pan and cook for 2 minutes on each side. Remove from the pan and set aside.

*4* Meanwhile, arrange the salad greens in a salad bowl, reserving a few for a garnish, and sprinkle over the onion, beet, radishes, and walnut halves.

*5* Put the walnut oil, mustard, lemon juice, salt, and pepper in a screw-top jar and shake until well blended. Pour over the salad and sprinkle with the sesame seeds.

*6* Arrange the mango and the salad on a serving plate, top with the chicken breast and garnish with a few of the salad greens.

# gingered chicken & vegetable salad

## ingredients

### serves 4

4 skinless, boneless chicken breasts
4 scallions, chopped
1-inch/2.5-cm piece fresh ginger,
    finely chopped
2 garlic cloves, crushed
2 tbsp vegetable or peanut oil

### salad

1 tbsp vegetable or peanut oil
1 onion, sliced
2 garlic cloves, chopped
4 oz/115 g baby corn, halved
4 oz/115 g snow peas, halved
    lengthwise
1 red bell pepper, seeded
    and sliced
3-inch/7.5-cm piece cucumber,
    peeled, seeded, and sliced
4 tbsp Thai soy sauce
1 tbsp jaggery or soft light
    brown sugar
few Thai basil leaves
6 oz/175 g fine egg noodles

## method

1 Cut the chicken into large cubes, each about 1 inch.
Mix the scallions, ginger, garlic, and oil together
in a shallow dish and add the chicken. Cover and let
marinate for at least 3 hours. Lift the meat out of
the marinade and set aside.

2 To make the salad, heat the oil in a wok or large skillet
and cook the onion for 1–2 minutes before adding the
rest of the vegetables, except the cucumber. Cook for
2–3 minutes, until just tender. Add the cucumber, half
the soy sauce, the sugar, and the basil, and mix gently.

3 Meanwhile, soak the noodles for 2–3 minutes (check
the package instructions) or until tender, and drain
well. Sprinkle the remaining soy sauce over them and
arrange on plates. Top with the cooked vegetables.

4 Add a little more oil to the wok, if necessary, and cook
the chicken over fairly high heat until browned on all
sides. Arrange the chicken cubes on top of the salad
and serve hot or warm.

# red chicken salad

## ingredients

### serves 4

4 boneless chicken breasts
2 tbsp red curry paste
2 tbsp vegetable or peanut oil
1 head Napa cabbage, shredded
6 oz/175 g bok choy, torn into
    large pieces
½ savoy cabbage, shredded
2 shallots, finely chopped
2 garlic cloves, crushed
1 tbsp rice wine vinegar
2 tbsp sweet chili sauce
2 tbsp Thai soy sauce

## method

1 Slash the flesh of the chicken several times and rub the curry paste into each cut. Cover and let chill overnight.

2 Cook in a heavy-bottom pan over medium heat or on a grill pan for 5–6 minutes, turning once or twice, until cooked through. Keep warm.

3 Heat 1 tablespoon of the oil in a wok or large skillet and stir-fry the Napa cabbage, bok choy, and savoy cabbage until just wilted. Add the remaining oil, shallots, and garlic, and stir-fry until just tender, but not browned. Add the vinegar, chili sauce, and soy. Remove from the heat.

4 Arrange the leaves on 4 serving plates. Slice the chicken, arrange on the greens, and drizzle the hot dressing over. Serve immediately.

# thai chicken salad

## ingredients

*serves 6*

vegetable oil spray
4 oz/115g skinless chicken breast,
 cut lengthwise horizontally
3 limes

### dressing

1 tbsp finely shredded lemongrass
1 small green chile, finely chopped
3 tbsp lime juice
½-inch/1-cm fresh ginger, peeled
 and thinly sliced into strips
1½ tsp sugar
2 tbsp white wine vinegar
3 fl oz/90 ml/⅓ cup water
1½ tsp cornstarch

### salad

1 oz/25 g rice vermicelli noodles
1¼ oz/50 g bell peppers, seeded
1¼ oz/50 g carrot
1¼ oz/50 g zucchini
1¼ oz/50 g snow peas
1¼ oz/50 g baby corn
1¼ oz/50 g broccoli florets
1¼ oz/50 g bok choy
4 tbsp roughly chopped fresh
 cilantro leaves

## method

*1* To make the dressing, put all the dressing ingredients, except the cornstarch, into a small pan over low heat and bring to a boil. Blend the cornstarch with a little cold water, gradually add to the pan, stirring continuously, and cook until thickened. Remove from the heat and let cool.

*2* Heat a grill pan over high heat and spray lightly with oil. Add the chicken and cook for 2 minutes on each side, or until thoroughly cooked through. Remove the chicken from the pan and shred.

*3* To make the salad, cover the rice vermicelli with boiling water then let it cool in the water. Meanwhile, finely slice the bell peppers, carrot, zucchini, snow peas, and baby corn into strips. Cut the broccoli florets into ¼-inch/5-mm pieces and shred the bok choy. Drain the rice vermicelli and put all the salad ingredients with the chicken into a large bowl. Pour over the dressing and toss together, making sure that all the ingredients are well coated.

*4* Cover and refrigerate for at least 2 hours before serving. Serve with the juice from half a lime squeezed over each portion.

# lunch & light meals

# spicy tomato chicken

## ingredients

### serves 4

1 lb 2 oz/500 g skinless, boneless
    chicken breasts
3 tbsp tomato paste
2 tbsp honey
2 tbsp Worcestershire sauce
1 tbsp chopped fresh rosemary
9 oz/250 g cherry tomatoes
fresh rosemary sprigs, to garnish
freshly cooked couscous or rice,
    to serve

## method

1 Using a sharp knife, cut the chicken into 1-inch/2.5-cm chunks and place in a bowl. Mix the tomato paste, honey, Worcestershire sauce, and rosemary together in a separate bowl, then add to the chicken, stirring to coat evenly.

2 Soak 8 wooden skewers in a bowl of cold water for 30 minutes to prevent them burning during cooking. Preheat the broiler to medium. Thread the chicken pieces and cherry tomatoes alternately onto the skewers and place on a broiler rack.

3 Spoon over any remaining glaze and cook under the preheated hot broiler for 8–10 minutes, turning occasionally, until the chicken is cooked through. Transfer to 4 large serving plates, garnish with a few sprigs of fresh rosemary, and serve with freshly cooked couscous or rice.

# hot & spicy chicken with peanuts

## ingredients

*serves 4*

**marinade**

2 tbsp soy sauce
1 tsp chili powder (or to taste)

**stir-fry**

12 oz/350 g skinless, boneless
    chicken breasts, cut into chunks
4 tbsp vegetable oil
1 garlic clove, finely chopped
1 tsp grated fresh ginger
3 shallots, thinly sliced
1½ cups carrots, thinly sliced
1 tsp white wine vinegar
pinch of sugar
3¼ oz/90 g/scant ⅔ cup
    roasted peanuts
1 tbsp peanut oil
cooked rice and cilantro sprigs,
    to serve

## method

1 To make the marinade, mix the soy sauce and chili powder in a bowl. Add the chicken chunks and toss to coat. Cover with plastic wrap and refrigerate for 30 minutes.

2 Heat the vegetable oil in a wok or skillet, and stir-fry the chicken until browned and well cooked. Remove from the wok then set aside and keep warm.

3 If necessary, add a little more oil to the wok, then add the garlic, ginger, shallots, and carrots. Stir-fry for 2–3 minutes.

4 Return the chicken to the wok and fry until it is warmed through. Add the vinegar, sugar, and peanuts, then stir well and drizzle with the peanut oil.

5 Serve immediately with freshly cooked rice and cilantro sprigs.

# chicken satay

## ingredients

### serves 4

2 tbsp vegetable or peanut oil
1 tbsp sesame oil
juice of ½ lime
2 skinless, boneless chicken
   breasts, cut into small cubes

### dip

2 tbsp vegetable or peanut oil
1 small onion, finely chopped
1 small fresh green chile, seeded
   and chopped
1 garlic clove, finely chopped
4 oz/115 g/½ cup crunchy
   peanut butter
6–8 tbsp water
juice of ½ lime

## method

1 Combine both the oils and the lime juice in a nonmetallic dish. Add the chicken cubes, cover with plastic wrap, and let chill for 1 hour. Soak 8–12 wooden skewers in cold water for 30 minutes before use, to prevent burning.

2 To make the dip, heat the oil in a skillet and sauté the onion, chile, and garlic over low heat, stirring occasionally, for about 5 minutes, until just softened. Add the peanut butter, water, and lime juice and let simmer gently, stirring constantly, until the peanut butter has softened enough to make a dip—you may need to add extra water to make a thinner consistency.

3 Meanwhile, drain the chicken cubes and thread them onto the wooden skewers. Put under a hot broiler or on a barbecue, turning frequently, for about 10 minutes, until cooked and browned. Serve hot with the warm dip.

# five-spice chicken with vegetables

## ingredients

### serves 4

2 tbsp sesame oil
1 garlic clove, chopped
3 scallions, trimmed and sliced
1 tbsp cornstarch
2 tbsp rice wine
4 skinless, boneless chicken
    breasts, cut into strips
1 tbsp Chinese five-spice powder
1 tbsp grated fresh ginger
4 fl oz/125 ml/½ cup chicken stock
3½ oz/100 g baby corn cobs, sliced
10½ oz/300 g/3 cups beansprouts
finely chopped scallions,
    to garnish, optional
freshly cooked jasmine rice,
    to serve

## method

1 Heat the oil in a preheated wok or large skillet. Add the garlic and scallions and stir-fry over medium-high heat for 1 minute.

2 In a bowl, mix together the cornstarch and rice wine, then add the mixture to the pan. Stir-fry for 1 minute, then add the chicken, five-spice powder, ginger, and chicken stock and cook for another 4 minutes. Add the corn cobs and cook for 2 minutes, then add the beansprouts and cook for another minute.

3 Remove from the heat, garnish with chopped scallions, if using, and serve with freshly cooked jasmine rice.

# sweet-&-sour chicken

## ingredients

### serves 4–6

1 lb/450 g lean chicken meat, cubed
5 tbsp vegetable or peanut oil
½ tsp minced garlic
½ tsp finely chopped fresh ginger
1 green bell pepper, coarsely chopped
1 onion, coarsely chopped
1 carrot, finely sliced
1 tsp sesame oil
1 tbsp finely chopped scallion
freshly cooked rice, to serve

### marinade

2 tsp light soy sauce
1 tsp Shaoxing rice wine
pinch of white pepper
½ tsp salt
dash of sesame oil

### sauce

8 tbsp rice vinegar
4 tbsp sugar
2 tsp light soy sauce
6 tbsp tomato ketchup

## method

1 Place all the marinade ingredients in a bowl and marinate the chicken pieces for at least 20 minutes.

2 To prepare the sauce, heat the vinegar in a pan and add the sugar, light soy sauce, and tomato ketchup. Stir to dissolve the sugar, then set aside.

3 In a preheated wok or deep pan, heat 3 tablespoons of the oil and stir-fry the chicken until it starts to turn golden brown. Remove and set aside.

4 In the clean wok or deep pan, heat the remaining oil and cook the garlic and ginger until fragrant. Add the vegetables and cook for 2 minutes. Add the chicken and cook for 1 minute. Finally add the sauce and sesame oil, then stir in the scallion and serve with rice.

# chicken with bok choy

## ingredients

*serves 4*

6 oz/175 g broccoli
1 tbsp peanut oil
1-inch/2.5-cm piece fresh ginger,
    finely grated
1 fresh red Thai chile, seeded
    and chopped
2 garlic cloves, crushed
1 red onion, cut into wedges
1 lb/450 g skinless, boneless
    chicken breast, cut into
    thin strips
6 oz/175 g bok choy, shredded
4 oz/115 g baby corn, halved
1 tbsp light soy sauce
1 tbsp Thai fish sauce
1 tbsp chopped fresh cilantro
1 tbsp toasted sesame seeds

## method

1 Break the broccoli into small florets and cook in a pan
   of lightly salted boiling water for 3 minutes. Drain and
   set aside.

2 Heat a wok over high heat until almost smoking, add
   the oil, and then add the ginger, chile, and garlic.
   Stir-fry for 1 minute. Add the onion and chicken and
   stir-fry for an additional 3–4 minutes, or until the
   chicken is sealed on all sides.

3 Add the remaining vegetables to the wok, including
   the broccoli, and stir-fry for 3–4 minutes, or until
   tender.

4 Add the soy and Thai fish sauces to the wok and stir-fry
   for an additional 1–2 minutes, then serve at once
   sprinkled with the cilantro and sesame seeds.

# creamy chicken curry with lemon rice

## ingredients

### serves 4

2 tbsp vegetable oil
4 skinless, boneless chicken
    breasts, 1 lb 12 oz/800 g, cut
    into 1-inch/2.5-cm pieces
1½ tsp cumin seeds
1 large onion, grated
2 fresh green chiles, finely chopped
2 large garlic cloves, grated
1 tbsp grated fresh ginger
1 tsp ground turmeric
1 tsp ground coriander
1 tsp garam masala
10 fl oz/300 ml/1¼ cups
    coconut milk
9 fl oz/250 ml chopped tomatoes
2 tsp lemon juice
2 tbsp chopped fresh cilantro,
    to garnish

### lemon rice

12 oz/350 g/scant 1¾ cups
    basmati rice, rinsed
40 fl oz/1.25 liters/5 cups water
juice and grated rind of 1 lemon
3 cloves

## method

1  Heat the oil in a large, heavy-bottom pan over medium heat. Add the chicken and cook for 5–8 minutes, until lightly browned and cooked through. Remove from the pan and set aside. Add the cumin seeds and cook until they start to darken and sizzle. Stir in the onion, partially cover, and cook over medium-low heat, stirring frequently, for 10 minutes, or until soft and golden. Add the chiles, garlic, ginger, turmeric, ground coriander, and garam masala and cook for 1 minute.

2  Return the chicken to the pan and stir in the coconut milk and tomatoes. Partially cover and cook for 15 minutes until the sauce has reduced and thickened. Stir in the lemon juice and season with salt.

3  Meanwhile, cook the rice. Put the rice into a pan and cover with the water. Add the lemon juice and cloves. Bring to a boil, then reduce the heat, cover, and let simmer over very low heat for 15 minutes, or until the rice is tender and all the water has been absorbed. Remove the pan from the heat and stir in the lemon rind. Let the rice stand, covered, for 5 minutes.

4  Serve the curry with the lemon rice, sprinkled with fresh cilantro.

# thai green chicken curry

## ingredients

*serves 4*

2 tbsp peanut or corn oil
2 tbsp Thai Green Curry Paste
1 lb 2 oz/500 g skinless, boneless
    chicken breasts, cut into cubes
2 kaffir lime leaves, roughly torn
1 lemongrass stalk, finely chopped
8 fl oz/225 ml/1 cup coconut milk
16 baby eggplants, halved
2 tbsp Thai fish sauce
sprigs of fresh Thai basil and thinly
    sliced kaffir lime leaves,
    to garnish

## method

*1* Heat the oil in a preheated wok or large, heavy-bottom skillet. Add the curry paste and stir-fry briefly until all the aromas are released.

*2* Add the chicken, lime leaves, and lemongrass and stir-fry for 3–4 minutes, until the meat is beginning to color. Add the coconut milk and eggplants and simmer gently for 8–10 minutes, or until tender.

*3* Stir in the fish sauce and serve immediately garnished with sprigs of Thai basil and lime leaves.

## variation

Replace the baby eggplants with 3 green bell peppers, sliced, which will enhance the green color of the curry.

# chicken breasts with coconut milk

## ingredients

*serves 4*

1 small onion, chopped

1 fresh green chile, seeded and chopped

1-inch/2.5-cm piece fresh ginger, chopped

2 tsp ground coriander

1 tsp ground cumin

1 tsp fennel seeds

1 tsp ground star anise

1 tsp cardamom seeds

½ tsp ground turmeric

½ tsp black peppercorns

½ tsp ground cloves

20 fl oz/625 ml/2½ cups canned coconut milk

4 skinless, boneless chicken breasts

vegetable oil, for brushing

fresh cilantro sprigs, to garnish

tomato rice and naan bread, to serve

## method

1 Place the onion, chile, ginger, coriander, cumin, fennel seeds, star anise, cardamom seeds, turmeric, peppercorns, cloves, and 16 fl oz/500 ml/2 cups of the coconut milk in a food processor and process to make a paste, adding more coconut milk if necessary.

2 Using a sharp knife, slash the chicken breasts several times and place in a large, shallow, nonmetallic dish in a single layer. Pour over half the coconut milk mixture and turn to coat completely. Cover with plastic wrap and let marinate in the refrigerator for at least 1 hour, and up to 8 hours.

3 Heat a ridged grill pan and brush lightly with vegetable oil. Add the chicken, in batches if necessary, and cook for 6–7 minutes on each side, or until tender.

4 Meanwhile, pour the remaining coconut milk mixture into a pan and bring to a boil, stirring occasionally. Arrange the chicken in a warmed serving dish, spoon over a little of the coconut sauce, and garnish with cilantro sprigs. Serve hot with tomato rice and naan bread.

# balti chicken

## ingredients

### serves 6

3 tbsp ghee or vegetable oil
2 large onions, sliced
3 tomatoes, sliced
½ tsp nigella seeds
4 black peppercorns
2 cardamom pods
1 cinnamon stick
1 tsp chili powder
1 tsp garam masala
1 tsp garlic paste
1 tsp ginger paste
salt
1 lb 9 oz/700 g skinless, boneless
    chicken breasts or thighs, diced
2 tbsp plain yogurt
2 tbsp chopped fresh cilantro,
    plus extra to garnish
2 fresh green chiles, seeded
    and finely chopped
2 tbsp lime juice
naan bread, to serve

## method

1 Heat the ghee in a large, heavy-bottom skillet. Add the onions and cook over low heat, stirring occasionally, for 10 minutes, or until golden. Add the sliced tomatoes, kalonji seeds, peppercorns, cardamoms, cinnamon stick, chili powder, garam masala, garlic paste, and ginger paste and season with salt. Cook, stirring constantly, for 5 minutes.

2 Add the chicken and cook, stirring constantly, for 5 minutes, or until well coated in the spice paste. Stir in the yogurt. Cover and let simmer, stirring occasionally, for 10 minutes.

3 Stir in the chopped cilantro, chiles, and lime juice. Transfer to a warmed serving dish, sprinkle with more chopped cilantro, and serve immediately with naan bread.

# lime chicken with mint

## ingredients

### serves 6

3 tbsp finely chopped fresh mint
4 tbsp honey
4 tbsp lime juice
salt and pepper
12 boneless chicken thighs
mixed salad, to serve

### sauce

5 fl oz/150 ml/²/₃ cup
    lowfat thick plain yogurt
1 tbsp finely chopped
    fresh mint
2 tsp finely grated lime rind

## method

1 Mix the mint, honey, and lime juice in a large bowl and season with salt and pepper. Use toothpicks to keep the chicken thighs in neat shapes and add the chicken to the marinade, turning to coat evenly.

2 Cover with plastic wrap and let the chicken marinate in the refrigerator for at least 30 minutes. Remove the chicken from the marinade and drain. Set aside the marinade.

3 Preheat the broiler to medium. Place the chicken on a broiler rack and cook under the hot broiler for 15–18 minutes, or until the chicken is tender and the juices run clear when the tip of a knife is inserted into the thickest part of the meat, turning the chicken frequently and basting with the marinade.

4 Meanwhile, combine all the sauce ingredients in a bowl. Remove the toothpicks and serve with a mixed salad and the sauce, for dipping.

# chicken with sesame sauce

## ingredients

### serves 4

12 oz/350 g boneless, skinless
    chicken meat
few drops of sesame oil
2 tbsp sesame paste
1 tbsp light soy sauce
1 tbsp chicken stock
½ tsp salt
pinch of sugar
8 tbsp shredded lettuce leaves
1 tbsp sesame seeds, roasted,
    to serve

## method

1 Place the chicken in a pan of cold water, then bring to a
  boil and let simmer for 8–10 minutes. Drain and let cool
  a little, then cut or tear the chicken into bite-size pieces.

2 Mix together the sesame oil, sesame paste, light soy
  sauce, chicken stock, salt, and sugar and whisk until the
  sauce is thick and smooth. Toss in the chicken.

3 To serve, put the shredded lettuce on a large plate and
  spoon the chicken and sauce on top. Sprinkle with the
  sesame seeds and serve at room temperature.

# thai spiced chicken with zucchini

## ingredients

*serves 4*

1 tbsp olive oil

1 garlic clove, finely chopped

1-inch/2.5-cm piece fresh ginger, peeled and finely chopped

1 small fresh red chile, seeded and finely chopped

12 oz/350 g skinless, boneless chicken breasts, cut into thin strips

1 tbsp Thai 7-spice seasoning

1 red bell pepper and 1 yellow bell pepper, seeded and sliced

2 zucchini, thinly sliced

8 oz/225 g canned bamboo shoots, drained

2 tbsp dry sherry or apple juice

1 tbsp light soy sauce

2 tbsp chopped fresh cilantro, plus extra to garnish

salt and pepper

## method

1 Heat the olive oil in a nonstick wok or large skillet. Add the garlic, ginger, and chile and stir-fry for 30 seconds to release the flavors.

2 Add the chicken and Thai seasoning and stir-fry for about 4 minutes or until the chicken has colored all over. Add the peppers and zucchini and stir-fry for 1–2 minutes, or until slightly softened.

3 Stir in the bamboo shoots and stir-fry for another 2–3 minutes, or until the chicken is cooked through and tender. Add the sherry or apple juice, soy sauce, and seasoning and sizzle for 1–2 minutes.

4 Stir in the chopped cilantro and serve immediately, garnished with extra cilantro.

# bacon-wrapped chicken burgers

## ingredients

*serves 4*

1 lb/450 g fresh ground chicken
1 onion, grated
2 garlic cloves, crushed
2 oz/55 g/⅜ cup pine nuts, toasted
2 oz/55 g Gruyère cheese, grated
2 tbsp fresh snipped chives
2 tbsp whole wheat flour
8 lean Canadian bacon slices
1–2 tbsp corn oil
salt and pepper
mayonnaise and chopped scallions
    (green part only), to garnish
crusty rolls, chopped lettuce and
    red onion rings, to serve

## method

1 Place the ground chicken, onion, garlic, pine nuts, cheese, chives, and salt and pepper in a food processor. Using the pulse button, blend the mixture together using short sharp bursts. Scrape out onto a board and shape into 4 even-size burgers. Coat in the flour, then cover and let chill for 1 hour.

2 Wrap each burger with 2 bacon slices, securing in place with a wooden toothpick.

3 Heat a heavy-bottom skillet and add the oil. When hot, add the burgers and cook over medium heat for 5–6 minutes on each side, or until thoroughly cooked through.

4 Serve the burgers immediately in crusty rolls on a bed of lettuce and red onion rings and top with mayonnaise and scallions.

# chicken fajitas

## ingredients

### serves 4

3 tbsp olive oil, plus extra
    for drizzling
3 tbsp maple syrup or honey
1 tbsp red wine vinegar
2 garlic cloves, crushed
2 tsp dried oregano
1–2 tsp dried chili flakes
4 skinless, boneless chicken breasts
2 red bell peppers, seeded and cut
    into 1-inch/2.5-cm strips
8 flour tortillas, warmed
salt and pepper
guacamole, to serve

## method

1 Place the oil, maple syrup, vinegar, garlic, oregano, chili
  flakes, salt, and pepper in a large, shallow plate or bowl
  and mix together.

2 Slice the chicken across the grain into slices 1 inch/
  2.5 cm thick. Toss in the marinade until well coated.
  Cover and let chill in the refrigerator for 2–3 hours,
  turning occasionally.

3 Heat a grill pan until hot. Lift the chicken slices from
  the marinade with a slotted spoon, lay on the grill pan,
  and cook over medium-high heat for 3–4 minutes
  on each side, or until cooked through. Remove the
  chicken to a warmed serving plate and keep warm.

4 Add the bell peppers, skin-side down, to the grill pan,
  and cook for 2 minutes on each side. Transfer to the
  serving plate.

5 Serve at once with guacamole, in the warmed tortillas.

# chicken wraps

## ingredients

*serves 4*

5 fl oz/150 ml/generous
⅔ cup lowfat plain yogurt
1 tbsp whole-grain mustard
10 oz/280 g cooked skinless,
boneless chicken breast, diced
5 oz/140 g iceberg lettuce, finely
shredded
3 oz/85 g cucumber, thinly sliced
2 celery stalks, sliced
3 oz/85 g/½ cup black seedless
grapes, halved
8 x 8-inch/20-cm soft flour
tortillas or 4 x 10-inch/
25-cm soft flour tortillas
pepper

## method

1 Combine the yogurt and mustard in a bowl and
season with pepper. Stir in the chicken and toss until
thoroughly coated.

2 Put the lettuce, cucumber, celery, and grapes into a
separate bowl and mix well.

3 Fold a tortilla in half and in half again to make a cone
that is easy to hold. Half-fill the tortilla pocket with
the salad mixture and top with some of the chicken
mixture. Repeat with the remaining tortillas, salad,
and chicken. Serve at once.

# filo chicken pie

## ingredients

### serves 6–8

3 lb 5 oz/1.5 kg whole chicken

1 small onion, halved, and 3 large onions, finely chopped

1 carrot, thickly sliced

1 celery stalk, thickly sliced

pared zest of 1 lemon

1 bay leaf

10 peppercorns

5½ oz/155 g butter

2 oz/55 g/scant ½ cup all-purpose flour

5 fl oz/150 ml/⅔ cup milk

1 oz/25 g/⅓ cup kefalotiri or romano cheese, grated

3 eggs, beaten

8 oz/225 g filo pastry (work with one sheet at a time and keep the remaining sheets covered with a damp dish towel)

salt and pepper

## method

1 Put the chicken in a large pan with the halved onion, carrot, celery, lemon zest, bay leaf, and peppercorns. Add cold water to cover and bring to a boil. Cover and simmer for about 1 hour, or until the chicken is cooked.

2 Remove the chicken and set aside to cool. Bring the stock to a boil and boil until reduced to about 20 fl oz/ 625 ml/2½ cups. Strain and reserve the stock. Cut the cooled chicken into pieces, without the skin and bones.

3 Fry the chopped onions until softened in 2 oz/55 g of the butter. Add the flour and cook gently, stirring, for 1–2 minutes. Gradually stir in the reserved stock and the milk. Bring to a boil, stirring constantly, then simmer for 1–2 minutes until thick and smooth. Remove from the heat, add the chicken, and season. Let cool, then stir in the cheese and eggs.

4 Melt the remaining butter and use a little to grease a deep 12 x 8-inch/30 x 20-cm metal baking pan. Cut the pastry sheets in half widthwise. Line the pan with one sheet of pastry and brush it with melted butter. Repeat with half of the pastry sheets. Spread the filling over the pastry, then top with the pastry sheets, brushing each with butter and tucking down the edges.

5 Bake in a preheated oven, 375°F/190°C, for about 50 minutes, until golden. Serve warm.

# pan-fried chicken & cilantro

## ingredients

### serves 4

1 tbsp corn oil

4 skinless, boneless chicken
    breasts, about 4 oz/115 g each,
    trimmed of all visible fat

1 tsp cornstarch

1 tbsp water

3 fl oz/90 ml/⅓ cup lowfat plain
    yogurt

2 tbsp reduced fat light cream

6 fl oz/175 ml/¾ cup chicken stock

2 tbsp lime juice

2 garlic cloves, finely chopped

1 shallot, finely chopped

1 tomato, peeled, seeded,
    and chopped

1 bunch of fresh cilantro, coarsely
    chopped, with extra to garnish

salt and pepper

## method

1 Heat the corn oil in a heavy-bottom skillet, add the
   chicken and cook over medium heat for 5 minutes on
   each side, or until the juices run clear when the meat is
   pierced with the tip of a sharp knife. Remove from the
   skillet and keep warm.

2 Mix the cornstarch and water until smooth. Stir in the
   yogurt and cream. Pour the chicken stock and lime
   juice into the skillet and add the garlic and shallot.
   Reduce the heat and let simmer for 1 minute. Stir the
   tomato into the yogurt mixture and stir the mixture
   into the skillet. Season with salt and pepper. Cook,
   stirring constantly, for 1–2 minutes, or until slightly
   thickened, but do not let the mixture boil. Stir in the
   chopped fresh cilantro.

3 Place the chicken on a large serving plate, pour the
   sauce over it and garnish with the reserved cilantro
   sprigs. Serve.

# chicken kabobs
# with yogurt sauce

## ingredients

### serves 4

10 fl oz/300 ml/1¼ cups strained
    plain yogurt
2 garlic cloves, crushed
juice of ½ lemon
1 tbsp chopped fresh herbs such
    as oregano, dill, tarragon,
    or parsley
4 large skinless, boneless chicken
    breasts
oil, for oiling
8 firm stems of fresh rosemary,
    optional
salt and pepper
lemon wedges, to garnish
shredded romaine lettuce
    and rice, to serve

## method

*1* To make the sauce, put the yogurt, garlic, lemon juice,
   herbs, salt, and pepper in a large bowl and mix well
   together.

*2* Cut the chicken breasts into chunks measuring about
   1½ inches/4 cm square. Add to the yogurt mixture and
   toss well together until the chicken pieces are coated.
   Cover and leave to marinate in the refrigerator
   for about 1 hour. If you are using wooden skewers,
   soak them in cold water for 30 minutes before use.

*3* Preheat the broiler. Thread the pieces of chicken onto
   8 flat, oiled, metal kabob skewers, wooden skewers,
   or rosemary stems and place on an oiled broiler pan.

*4* Cook the kabobs under the broiler for about
   15 minutes, turning and basting with the remaining
   marinade occasionally, until lightly browned
   and tender.

*5* Pour the remaining marinade into a pan and heat
   gently but do not boil. Serve the kabobs with
   shredded lettuce on a bed of rice and garnish with
   lemon wedges. Accompany with the yogurt sauce.

# gingered chicken kabobs

## ingredients

*serves 4*

3 skinless, boneless chicken
    breasts, cut into small cubes
juice of 1 lime
1-inch/2.5-cm piece ginger,
    peeled and chopped
1 fresh red chile, seeded
    and sliced
2 tbsp vegetable or peanut oil
1 onion, sliced
2 garlic cloves, chopped
1 eggplant, cut into chunks
2 zucchini, cut into thick slices
1 red bell pepper, seeded and
    cut into squares
2 tbsp red curry paste
2 tbsp Thai soy sauce
1 tsp jaggery or soft light brown
    sugar
boiled rice, with chopped cilantro,
    to serve

## method

1 Put the chicken cubes in a shallow dish. Mix the lime, ginger, and chile together and pour over the chicken pieces. Stir gently to coat. Cover and let chill in the refrigerator for at least 3 hours to marinate.

2 Soak 8–12 wooden skewers in cold water for 30 minutes before use, to prevent burning.

3 Thread the chicken pieces onto the soaked wooden skewers and cook under a hot broiler for 3–4 minutes, turning frequently, until they are cooked through.

4 Meanwhile, heat the oil in a wok or large skillet and sauté the onion and garlic for 1–2 minutes, until softened, but not browned. Add the eggplant, zucchini, and bell pepper and cook for 3–4 minutes, until cooked but still firm. Add the curry paste, soy sauce, and sugar, and cook for 1 minute.

5 Divide the vegetables among serving plates and top with the kabobs. Serve hot with boiled rice, stirred through with chopped cilantro.

# asian-style glazed chicken wings

## ingredients

### serves 4

8 chicken wings, each wing
    chopped into 3 pieces
5 tbsp peanut oil
6 tbsp chicken stock or water
2 tbsp chopped fresh cilantro

### marinade

1½ tbsp Chinese rice wine
    or dry sherry
1 tbsp soy sauce
1 tbsp rice vinegar
1½ tbsp sugar
¼ tsp salt
⅛ tsp Chinese five-spice seasoning
3 tbsp hoisin.sauce
1 tsp finely chopped fresh ginger

## method

1 To make the marinade, combine the wine, soy sauce, and vinegar in a small bowl. Add the sugar, salt, and five-spice seasoning and stir until dissolved. Mix in the hoisin sauce and ginger.

2 Put the chopped chicken wings in a shallow dish and pour in the marinade, turning the wings to coat. Let stand to marinate for 1 hour at room temperature, or overnight in the refrigerator.

3 Heat a wok over a high heat, add the oil, and when it is almost smoking, add the chicken wings and marinade. Stir-fry for 5 minutes, then sprinkle with 4 tablespoons of the stock and stir-fry for another 4 minutes.

4 Using tongs, transfer the wings to a serving dish and sprinkle with the cilantro. Pour off and discard most of the oil from the wok and return to the heat. Add the remaining 2 tablespoons of stock and stir with a wooden spoon until blended, scraping up the sticky sediment. Pour into a small bowl and serve with the wings as a dipping sauce.

# hearty
# dishes

# traditional roast chicken

## ingredients

### serves 4

1 oz/25 g butter, softened
1 garlic clove, finely chopped
3 tbsp finely chopped
    toasted walnuts
1 tbsp chopped fresh parsley
salt and pepper
1 oven-ready chicken, weighing
    4 lb/1.8 kg
1 lime, cut into fourths
2 tbsp vegetable oil
1 tbsp cornstarch
2 tbsp water
lime wedges and fresh rosemary
    sprigs, to garnish
roast potatoes and a selection
    of freshly cooked vegetables,
    to serve

## method

1 Mix 1 tablespoon of the butter with the garlic, walnuts, and parsley together in a small bowl. Season well with salt and pepper. Loosen the skin from the breast of the chicken without breaking it. Spread the butter mixture evenly between the skin and breast meat. Place the lime fourths inside the body cavity.

2 Pour the oil into a roasting pan. Transfer the chicken to the pan and dot the skin with the remaining butter. Roast in a preheated oven, 375°F/190°C, for 1³⁄₄ hours, basting occasionally, until the chicken is tender and the juices run clear when a skewer is inserted into the thickest part of the meat. Lift out the chicken and place on a serving platter to rest for 10 minutes.

3 Blend the cornstarch with the water, then stir into the juices in the pan. Stir over low heat until thickened, adding more water if necessary. Garnish the chicken with lime wedges and rosemary sprigs. Serve with roast potatoes and a selection of freshly cooked vegetables and spoon over the thickened juices.

# chicken & barley stew

## ingredients

### serves 4

2 tbsp vegetable oil
8 small, skinless chicken thighs
generous 2 cups chicken stock
scant $\frac{1}{2}$ cup pearl barley, rinsed
    and drained
7 oz/200 g small new potatoes,
    scrubbed and cut in half
    lengthwise
2 large carrots, peeled and sliced
1 leek, trimmed and sliced
2 shallots, sliced
1 tbsp tomato paste
1 bay leaf
1 zucchini, trimmed and sliced
2 tbsp chopped fresh flat-leaf
    parsley, plus extra sprigs
    to garnish
2 tbsp all-purpose flour
4 tbsp water
salt and pepper

## method

1 Heat the oil in a large pot over medium heat. Add the chicken and cook for 3 minutes, then turn over and cook on the other side for another 2 minutes. Add the stock, barley, potatoes, carrots, leek, shallots, tomato paste, and bay leaf. Bring to a boil, lower the heat, and simmer for 30 minutes.

2 Add the zucchini and chopped parsley, cover the pan, and cook for another 20 minutes, or until the chicken is cooked through. Remove the bay leaf and discard.

3 In a separate bowl, mix the flour with the water and stir into a smooth paste. Add it to the stew and cook, stirring, over low heat for another 5 minutes. Season to taste with salt and pepper.

4 Remove from the heat, ladle into individual serving bowls, and garnish with sprigs of fresh parsley.

# chicken, tomato & onion casserole

## ingredients

### serves 4

1½ tbsp unsalted butter
2 tbsp olive oil
4 lb/1.8 kg skinned chicken
    drumsticks
2 red onions, sliced
2 garlic cloves, finely chopped
14 oz/400 g canned chopped
    tomatoes
2 tbsp chopped flat-leaf parsley,
    plus extra to garnish
6 fresh basil leaves, torn
1 tbsp sun-dried tomato paste
⅔ cup full-bodied red wine
3¼ cups sliced mushrooms
salt and pepper

## method

1 Heat the butter with the olive oil in a large flameproof casserole. Add the chicken drumsticks and cook, turning frequently, for 5–10 minutes, or until golden all over and sealed. Using a slotted spoon, transfer the drumsticks to a plate.

2 Add the onions and garlic to the casserole and cook over low heat, stirring occasionally, for 10 minutes, or until golden. Add the tomatoes, parsley, basil, tomato paste, and wine, and then season to taste with salt and pepper.

3 Bring to a boil, then return the chicken drumsticks to the casserole, pushing them down under the liquid. Cover and cook in a preheated oven, 325°F/160°C, for 50 minutes.

4 Add the mushrooms and cook for another 10 minutes, or until the chicken drumsticks are tender and the juices run clear when a skewer is inserted into the thickest part of the meat. Serve immediately, garnished with chopped parsley.

# spiced chicken stew

## ingredients

*serves 6*

4 lb/1.8 kg chicken parts
2 tbsp paprika
2 tbsp olive oil
2 tbsp butter
1 lb/450 g onions, chopped
2 yellow bell peppers, seeded
    and chopped
14 oz/400 g canned chopped
    tomatoes
8 fl oz/225 ml/scant 1 cup dry
    white wine
16 fl oz/450 ml/generous 1¼ cups
    chicken stock
1 tbsp Worcestershire sauce
½ tsp Tabasco sauce
1 tbsp finely chopped fresh parsley
11½ oz/325 g canned corn kernels,
    drained
15 oz/425 g canned lima beans,
    drained and rinsed
2 tbsp all-purpose flour
4 tbsp water
salt
fresh parsley sprigs, to garnish

## method

*1* Season the chicken parts with salt and dust with paprika.

*2* Heat the oil and butter in a flameproof casserole or large pan. Add the chicken parts and cook over medium heat, turning, for 10–15 minutes, or until golden. Transfer to a plate with a slotted spoon.

*3* Add the onion and bell peppers to the casserole. Cook over low heat, stirring occasionally, for 5 minutes, or until softened.

*4* Add the tomatoes, wine, stock, Worcestershire sauce, Tabasco sauce, and parsley and bring to a boil, stirring. Return the chicken to the casserole, cover, and simmer, stirring occasionally, for 30 minutes.

*5* Add the corn and beans to the casserole, partially re-cover, and simmer for an additional 30 minutes. Place the flour and water in a small bowl and mix to make a paste. Stir a ladleful of the cooking liquid into the paste, then stir the paste into the stew. Cook, stirring frequently, for 5 minutes. Serve, garnished with parsley.

# roasted chicken with sun-blush tomato pesto

## ingredients

*serves 4*

4 skinless, boneless chicken
   breasts, about 1 lb 12 oz/
   800 g in total
1 tbsp olive oil
salt and pepper
2 tbsp pine nuts, lightly toasted,
   to garnish

### pesto

4½ oz/125 g sun-blush tomatoes
   in oil (drained weight),
   chopped
2 garlic cloves, crushed
4 tbsp pine nuts, lightly toasted
5 fl oz/150 ml/⅔ cup extra virgin
   olive oil

## method

1 To make the red pesto, put the sun-blush tomatoes,
   garlic, 4 tablespoons of the pine nuts, and oil into
   a food processor and process to a coarse paste.

2 Arrange the chicken in a large, ovenproof dish or
   roasting pan. Brush each breast with the oil, then place
   a tablespoon of red pesto over each breast. Using the
   back of a spoon, spread the pesto so that it covers
   the top of each breast. (Store the remaining pesto in an
   airtight container in the refrigerator for up to 1 week.)

3 Roast the chicken in a preheated oven, 400°F/200°C
   for 30 minutes, or until tender and the juices run clear
   when a skewer is inserted into the thickest part of
   the meat.

4 Serve sprinkled with toasted pine nuts.

## variation

Add 12 stoned and finely chopped black olives (well
drained and rinsed) and ½ tablespoon olive oil to the
pesto after processing; stir well.

# roast cinnamon squab chickens with lentils

## ingredients

### serves 4

4 squab chickens, about
    1 lb 2 oz/500 g each
2 tbsp maple syrup
1 tsp ground cinnamon
1 tbsp vegetable oil
3½ fl oz/100 ml/generous ⅓ cup
    low-salt chicken stock
2 red onions, sliced
1 tsp cumin seeds
1 tsp coriander seeds
1 tbsp olive oil
2 garlic cloves, crushed
1 lb 12 oz/800 g canned lentils,
    drained and rinsed
1 tbsp unsalted butter
2 tbsp chopped fresh parsley
pepper
steamed broccoli or green beans,
    to serve (optional)

## method

*1* Arrange the squab chickens in a roasting pan. Mix the maple syrup, cinnamon, and vegetable oil together in a small bowl and brush over the breasts of the squab chickens. Pour the stock into the roasting pan and tuck the onion slices around the birds. Roast in a preheated oven, 375°F/190°C, for 35 minutes.

*2* Meanwhile, heat a nonstick skillet over medium heat, add the cumin and coriander seeds, and cook, turning, until they start to give off an aroma. Tip into a mortar and finely crush with a pestle.

*3* Heat the olive oil in a skillet over low heat, add the garlic and spices, and cook for 1–2 minutes, stirring constantly. Add the lentils and cook for 10–15 minutes, stirring occasionally.

*4* Remove the chicken from the oven, and keep warm. Put the roasting pan on the stove and bring the cooking juices up to a simmer. Stir in the butter and half the parsley. Season with pepper.

*5* To serve, divide the lentils among 4 warmed serving plates. Add a squab chicken to each plate, pour over the sauce, and sprinkle with the remaining parsley. Serve with steamed broccoli or green beans, if liked.

# sticky lime chicken

## ingredients

*serves 4*

4 part-boned, skinless chicken
    breasts, about 5 oz/140 g each
grated rind and juice of 1 lime
1 tbsp honey
1 tbsp olive oil
1 garlic clove, chopped (optional)
1 tbsp chopped fresh thyme
pepper
boiled new potatoes and
    lightly cooked seasonal
    vegetables, to serve

## method

1 Arrange the chicken breasts in a shallow roasting pan.

2 Put the lime rind and juice, honey, oil, garlic, if using, and thyme in a small bowl and combine thoroughly. Spoon the mixture evenly over the chicken breasts and season with pepper.

3 Roast the chicken in a preheated oven, 375°F/190°C, basting every 10 minutes, for 35–40 minutes, or until the chicken is tender and the juices run clear when a skewer is inserted into the thickest part of the meat. If the juices still run pink, return the chicken to the oven and cook for an additional 5 minutes, then test again. As the chicken cooks, the liquid in the pan thickens to give a tasty, sticky coating.

4 Serve with boiled new potatoes and lightly cooked seasonal vegetables.

# chicken with saffron mash potatoes

## ingredients

### serves 4

1 lb 4 oz/550 g mealy potatoes,
    cut into chunks
1 garlic clove, peeled
1 tsp saffron threads, crushed
40 fl oz/1.25 liters/5 cups chicken
    or vegetable stock
4 skinless, boneless chicken
    breasts, trimmed of all
    visible fat
2 tbsp olive oil
1 tbsp lemon juice
1 tbsp chopped fresh thyme
1 tbsp chopped fresh cilantro
1 tbsp coriander seeds, crushed
3¹/₂ fl oz/100 ml/¹/₃ cup hot skim milk
salt and pepper
fresh thyme sprigs, to garnish

## method

1 Put the potatoes, garlic, and saffron in a large heavy-bottom pan, add the stock and bring to a boil. Cover and let simmer for 20 minutes, or until tender.

2 Meanwhile, brush the chicken breasts all over with half the olive oil and all of the lemon juice. Sprinkle with the fresh thyme, cilantro, and the crushed coriander seeds. Heat a griddle pan, add the chicken, and cook over medium–high heat for 5 minutes on each side, or until the juices run clear when the meat is pierced with the tip of a sharp knife. Alternatively, cook the chicken breasts under a preheated medium-hot broiler for 5 minutes on each side, or until cooked through.

3 Drain the potatoes and return the contents of the strainer to the pan. Add the remaining olive oil and the milk, season with salt and pepper, and mash until smooth. Divide the saffron mash among 4 large, warmed serving plates, top with a piece of chicken, and garnish with a few sprigs of fresh thyme. Serve.

# tarragon chicken

## ingredients

*serves 4*

4 skinless, boneless chicken
    breasts, about 6 oz/175 g each
4 fl oz/125 ml/½ cup
    dry white wine
8–10 fl oz/250–300 ml/
    1–1¼ cups chicken stock
1 garlic clove, finely chopped
1 tbsp dried tarragon
6 fl oz/175 ml/¾ cup heavy cream
1 tbsp chopped fresh tarragon
salt and pepper
fresh tarragon sprigs, to garnish

## method

1 Season the chicken with salt and pepper and place in
a single layer in a large, heavy-bottom skillet. Pour
in the wine and just enough chicken stock to cover,
and add the garlic and dried tarragon. Bring to a boil,
reduce the heat, and cook gently for 10 minutes,
or until the chicken is tender and cooked through.

2 Remove the chicken with a slotted spoon or tongs,
cover, and keep warm. Strain the poaching liquid into a
clean skillet and skim off any fat from the surface. Bring
to a boil and cook for 12–15 minutes, or until reduced
by about two-thirds.

3 Stir in the cream, return to a boil, and cook until
reduced by about half. Stir in the fresh tarragon. Slice
the chicken breasts and arrange on warmed plates.
Spoon over the sauce, garnish with tarragon sprigs,
and serve immediately.

# tuscan chicken

## ingredients

*serves 4*

2 tbsp all-purpose flour
4 skinned chicken parts
3 tbsp olive oil
1 red onion, chopped
2 garlic cloves, finely chopped
1 red bell pepper, seeded and
    chopped
pinch of saffron threads
5 fl oz/150 ml/²⁄₃ cup chicken stock
    or a mixture of chicken stock
    and dry white wine
14 oz/400 g canned tomatoes,
    chopped
4 sun-dried tomatoes in oil,
    drained and chopped
8 oz/225 g portobello mushrooms,
    sliced
4 oz/115 g/²⁄₃ cup black olives,
    pitted
4 tbsp lemon juice
salt and pepper
fresh basil leaves, to garnish
tagliatelle, fettuccine, or tagliarini
    and crusty bread, to serve

## method

1 Place the flour on a shallow plate and season with salt
and pepper. Coat the chicken in the seasoned flour,
shaking off any excess. Heat the olive oil in a large,
flameproof casserole. Add the chicken and cook over
medium heat, turning frequently, for 5–7 minutes,
until golden brown. Remove from the casserole and
set aside.

2 Add the onion, garlic, and red bell pepper to the
casserole, reduce the heat and cook, stirring
occasionally, for 5 minutes, until softened. Meanwhile,
stir the saffron into the stock.

3 Stir the tomatoes, with the juice from the can, and the
sun-dried tomatoes, mushrooms, and olives into the
casserole and cook, stirring occasionally, for 3 minutes.
Pour in the stock and saffron mixture and the lemon
juice. Bring to a boil, then return the chicken to the
casserole.

4 Cover and cook in a preheated oven, 350°F/180°C, for
1 hour, until the chicken is tender. Garnish with the
basil leaves and serve immediately with pasta and
crusty bread.

# chicken with goat cheese & basil

## ingredients

*serves 4*

4 skinless, boneless chicken breasts
3½ oz/100 g soft goat cheese
small bunch fresh basil
2 tbsp olive oil
salt and pepper

## method

1 Using a sharp knife, slit along one long edge of each chicken breast, then carefully open out each breast to make a small pocket. Divide the cheese equally among the pockets, and tuck three or four basil leaves in each. Close the openings and season the breasts with salt and pepper.

2 Heat the oil in a skillet, add the chicken breasts, and fry gently for 15–20 minutes, turning several times, until golden and tender.

3 Serve warm, garnished with a sprig of basil.

# chicken gumbo

## ingredients

### serves 4–6

3 lb 5 oz/1.5 kg chicken,
cut into 6 parts
2 celery stalks, 1 broken in half
and 1 finely chopped
1 carrot, chopped
2 onions, 1 sliced and 1 chopped
2 bay leaves
4 tbsp peanut oil
1¾ oz/50 g/⅓ cup all-purpose flour
2 large garlic cloves, crushed
1 green bell pepper, seeded
and diced
1 lb/450 g fresh okra, trimmed,
then cut crosswise into
½-inch/1-cm slices
8 oz/225 g andouille sausage
or Polish kielbasa, sliced
2 tbsp tomato paste
1 tsp dried thyme
½ tsp cayenne pepper
14 oz/400 g canned peeled
plum tomatoes
salt and pepper
cooked long-grain rice, to serve

## method

1 Put the chicken into a large pan with water to cover,
bring to the boil, skimming the surface to remove the
foam. Reduce the heat to medium, add the celery stalk
halves, carrot, sliced onion, 1 bay leaf, and ¼ teaspoon
of salt and simmer for 30 minutes, or until the chicken
is tender and the juices run clear when a skewer is
inserted into the thickest part of the meat. Remove the
chicken, straining and reserving 4 cups of the liquid.
Remove and discard the skin, bones, and other
ingredients. Cut the chicken flesh into bite-size pieces
and reserve.

2 Heat the oil in a large pan. Over a low heat, sprinkle
in the flour, and stir to make a roux. Add the chopped
celery, chopped onion, garlic, green bell pepper, and
okra to the pan. Increase the heat to medium–high and
cook, stirring frequently, for 5 minutes. Add the sausage
and cook, stirring frequently, for 2 minutes. Stir in all the
remaining ingredients, except the chicken, including
the second bay leaf and the reserved cooking liquid.

3 Bring to a boil, then reduce the heat to medium–low
and simmer, uncovered, for 30 minutes, stirring
occasionally. Add the chicken to the pan and simmer
for another 30 minutes. Taste and adjust the seasoning,
if necessary. Remove and discard the bay leaf, spoon
the gumbo over the rice, and serve.

# chicken in white wine

## ingredients

*serves 4*

4 tbsp butter
2 tbsp olive oil
2 slices rindless, thick bacon, chopped
4 oz/115 g pearl onions, peeled
1 garlic clove, finely chopped
4 lb/1.8 kg chicken parts
14 fl oz/400 ml/1¾ cups dry white wine
10 fl oz/300 ml/1¼ cups chicken stock
1 bouquet garni
4 oz/115 g button mushrooms
1 oz/25 g/3 tbsp all-purpose flour
salt and pepper
fresh mixed herbs, to garnish

## method

1 Melt half the butter with the oil in a flameproof casserole. Add the bacon and cook over medium heat, stirring, for 5–10 minutes, or until golden brown. Transfer the bacon to a large plate. Add the onions and garlic to the casserole and cook over low heat, stirring occasionally, for 10 minutes, or until golden. Transfer to the plate.

2 Add the chicken and cook over medium heat, stirring continuously, for 8–10 minutes, or until golden. Transfer to the plate. Drain off any excess fat. Stir in the wine and stock and bring to a boil, scraping any sediment off the bottom. Add the bouquet garni and season to taste with salt and pepper. Return the bacon, onions, and chicken to the casserole. Cover and cook in a preheated oven, 325°F/160°C, for 1 hour. Add the mushrooms, re-cover, and cook for 15 minutes. Meanwhile, make a beurre manié by mashing the remaining butter with the flour in a small bowl.

3 Remove the casserole from the oven and set over medium heat. Remove and discard the bouquet garni. Whisk in the beurre manié, a little at a time. Bring to a boil, stirring, then serve, garnished with fresh herb sprigs.

# chicken tagine

## ingredients

### serves 4

1 tbsp olive oil

1 onion, cut into small wedges

2–4 garlic cloves, sliced

1 lb/450 g skinless, boneless
   chicken breasts, diced

1 tsp ground cumin

2 cinnamon sticks, lightly bruised

1 tbsp plain whole-wheat flour

8 oz/225 g/2¼ cups diced
   eggplant

1 red bell pepper, seeded and
   chopped

3 oz/85 g/1¼ cups sliced button
   mushrooms

1 tbsp tomato paste

1 pint/600 ml/2½ cups chicken
   stock

10 oz/280 g canned chickpeas,
   drained and rinsed

2 oz/55 g/⅓ cup chopped dried
   apricots

salt and pepper

1 tbsp chopped fresh cilantro,
   to garnish

## method

1 Heat the oil in a large saucepan over medium heat,
   add the onion and garlic, and cook for 3 minutes,
   stirring frequently. Add the chicken and cook, stirring
   continuously, for another 5 minutes, or until sealed on
   all sides. Add the cumin and cinnamon sticks to the
   saucepan halfway through sealing the chicken.

2 Sprinkle in the flour and cook, stirring continuously,
   for 2 minutes. Add the eggplant, red bell pepper, and
   mushrooms and cook for another 2 minutes, stirring
   continuously. Blend the tomato paste with the stock,
   stir into the saucepan, and bring to a boil. Reduce the
   heat and add the chickpeas and apricots. Cover and
   simmer for 15–20 minutes, or until the chicken
   is tender.

3 Season with salt and pepper to taste and serve
   immediately, sprinkled with cilantro.

# florida chicken

## ingredients

*serves 4*

1 lb/450 g skinless, boneless chicken
1½ tbsp all-purpose flour
1 tbsp olive oil
1 onion, cut into wedges
2 celery stalks, sliced
5 fl oz/150 ml/⅔ cup orange juice
10 fl oz/300 ml/1¼ cups chicken stock
1 tbsp light soy sauce
1–2 tsp honey
1 tbsp grated orange rind
1 orange bell pepper, seeded and chopped
1 medium zucchini, sliced into half moons
2 small corn cobs, halved
1 orange, peeled and segmented
salt and pepper
1 tbsp chopped fresh parsley, to garnish

## method

1 Lightly rinse the chicken and pat dry with paper towels. Cut into bite-size pieces. Season the flour well with salt and pepper. Toss the chicken in the seasoned flour until well coated and reserve any remaining seasoned flour.

2 Heat the oil in a large heavy-bottom skillet and cook the chicken over high heat, stirring frequently, for 5 minutes, or until golden on all sides and sealed. Using a slotted spoon, transfer the chicken to a plate. Add the onion and celery to the skillet and cook over medium heat, stirring frequently, for 5 minutes, or until softened. Sprinkle in the reserved seasoned flour and cook, stirring continuously, for 2 minutes, then remove from the heat. Gradually stir in the orange juice, stock, soy sauce, and honey, followed by the orange rind, then return to the heat and bring to a boil, stirring.

3 Return the chicken to the skillet. Reduce the heat, cover, and simmer, stirring occasionally, for 15 minutes. Add the orange pepper, zucchini, and corn cobs and simmer for another 10 minutes, or until the chicken and vegetables are tender. Add the orange segments, stir well, and heat for 1 minute. Serve, garnished with the parsley.

# mexican chicken, chili & potato pot

## ingredients

*serves 4*

2 tbsp vegetable oil

1 lb/450 g skinless, boneless
chicken breasts, cubed

1 onion, finely chopped

1 green bell pepper, seeded
and finely chopped

1 potato, diced

1 sweet potato, diced

2 garlic cloves, very finely chopped

1–2 fresh green chiles, seeded
and finely chopped

7 oz/200 g canned chopped
tomatoes

½ tsp dried oregano

½ tsp salt

¼ tsp pepper

4 tbsp chopped fresh cilantro

2 cups chicken stock

## method

1 Heat the oil in a large heavy-bottom saucepan over medium–high heat. Add the chicken and cook until lightly browned. Reduce the heat to medium. Add the onion, bell pepper, potato, and sweet potato. Cover and cook, stirring occasionally, for 5 minutes, or until the vegetables begin to soften.

2 Add the garlic and chiles and cook for 1 minute. Stir in the tomatoes, oregano, salt, pepper, and half the cilantro and cook for 1 minute. Pour in the stock. Bring to a boil, then cover and simmer over a medium–low heat for 15–20 minutes, or until the chicken is cooked through and the vegetables are tender.

3 Sprinkle with the remaining cilantro just before serving.

# coq au vin

## ingredients

### serves 4

2 tbsp butter
8 baby onions
4½ oz/125 g bacon,
    roughly chopped
4 chicken parts
1 garlic clove, finely chopped
12 white mushrooms
10 fl oz/300 ml/1¼ cups red wine
bouquet garni sachet
1 tbsp chopped fresh tarragon
salt and pepper
2 tsp cornstarch
1–2 tbsp cold water
fresh flat-leaf parsley
    sprigs, to garnish
sautéed sliced potatoes,
    to serve

## method

1 Melt half of the butter in a large skillet over medium heat. Add the onions and bacon and cook, stirring, for 3 minutes. Lift out the bacon and onions and reserve.

2 Melt the remaining butter in the skillet and add the chicken parts. Cook for 3 minutes, then turn over and cook on the other side for 2 minutes. Drain off some of the chicken fat, then return the bacon and onions to the pan. Add the garlic, mushrooms, red wine, bouquet garni, and tarragon. Season with salt and pepper. Cook for about 1 hour, or until the chicken is cooked through.

3 Remove the skillet from the heat, lift out the chicken, onions, bacon, and mushrooms, transfer them to a serving platter, and keep the dish warm. Discard the bouquet garni.

4 Mix the cornstarch with enough of the water to make a paste, then stir into the juices in the skillet. Bring to a boil, reduce the heat, and cook, stirring, for 1 minute. Pour the sauce over the chicken, garnish with parsley sprigs, and serve with sautéed sliced potatoes.

# spanish chicken with preserved lemons

## ingredients

*serves 4*

1 tbsp all-purpose flour
4 chicken quarters, skin on
2 tbsp olive oil
2 garlic cloves, crushed
1 large Spanish onion, thinly sliced
24 fl oz/750 ml/3 cups
    low-salt chicken stock
½ tsp saffron threads
2 yellow bell peppers, seeded
    and cut into chunks
2 preserved lemons, cut into
    fourths
9 oz/250 g/generous 1¼ cups
    brown basmati rice
white pepper
12 pimiento-stuffed green olives
chopped fresh parsley,
    to garnish
salad greens, to serve

## method

*1* Put the flour into a large freezer bag. Add the chicken, close the top of the bag, and shake to coat with flour.

*2* Heat the oil in a large skillet over low heat, add the garlic, and cook for 1 minute, stirring constantly. Add the chicken to the skillet and cook over medium heat, turning frequently, for 5 minutes, or until the skin has lightly browned, then remove to a plate. Add the onion to the skillet and cook, stirring occasionally, for 10 minutes until soft.

*3* Meanwhile, put the stock and saffron into a pan over low heat and heat through.

*4* Transfer the chicken and onion to a large casserole dish, add the bell peppers, lemons, and rice, then pour over the stock. Mix well and season with pepper.

*5* Cover and cook in a preheated oven, 350°F/180°C, for 50 minutes, or until the chicken is cooked through and tender. Reduce the oven temperature to 325°F/160°C. Add the olives to the casserole and cook for an additional 10 minutes.

*6* Serve the dish sprinkled with chopped parsley and accompanied by salad greens.

# louisiana chicken

## ingredients

*serves 4*

5 tbsp corn oil
4 chicken parts
6 tbsp all-purpose flour
1 onion, chopped
2 celery stalks, sliced
1 green bell pepper, seeded
    and chopped
2 garlic cloves, finely chopped
2 tsp chopped fresh thyme
2 fresh red chiles, seeded
    and finely chopped
14 oz/400 g canned
    chopped tomatoes
10 fl oz/300 ml/1¼ cups chicken
    stock
salt and pepper
corn salad and chopped
    fresh thyme, to garnish

## method

*1* Heat the oil in a large, heavy-bottomed pan or flameproof casserole. Add the chicken and cook over medium heat, stirring, for 5–10 minutes, or until golden. Transfer the chicken to a plate with a perforated spoon.

*2* Stir the flour into the oil and cook over very low heat, stirring constantly, for 15 minutes, or until light golden. Do not let it burn. Add the onion, celery, and green bell pepper and cook, stirring constantly, for 2 minutes. Add the garlic, thyme, and chiles and cook, stirring, for 1 minute.

*3* Stir in the tomatoes and their juices, then gradually stir in the stock. Return the chicken pieces to the pan, cover, and simmer for 45 minutes, or until the chicken is cooked through and tender. Season with salt and pepper, transfer to warmed serving plates and serve immediately, garnished with some corn salad and a sprinkling of chopped thyme.

# red hot chili chicken

## ingredients

*serves 4*

1 tbsp curry paste
2 fresh green chiles, chopped
5 dried red chiles
2 tbsp tomato paste
2 garlic cloves, chopped
1 tsp chili powder
pinch of sugar
pinch of salt
2 tbsp peanut or corn oil
½ tsp cumin seeds
1 onion, chopped
2 curry leaves
1 tsp ground cumin
1 tsp ground coriander
½ tsp ground turmeric
14 oz/400 g canned chopped
    tomatoes
5 fl oz/150 ml/⅔ cup chicken stock
4 skinless, boneless chicken breasts
1 tsp garam masala
freshly cooked rice and plain
    yogurt garnished with mint
    sprigs and diced cucumber,
    to serve

## method

1 To make the chili paste, place the curry paste, fresh and dried chiles, tomato paste, garlic, chili powder, and sugar in a blender or food processor with the salt. Process to a smooth paste.

2 Heat the oil in a large, heavy-bottom pan. Add the cumin seeds and cook over medium heat, stirring constantly, for 2 minutes, or until they begin to pop and release their aroma. Add the onion and curry leaves and cook, stirring, for 5 minutes.

3 Add the chili paste, cook for 2 minutes, then stir in the ground cumin, coriander, and turmeric and cook for an additional 2 minutes.

4 Add the tomatoes and their juices and the stock. Bring to a boil, then reduce the heat and simmer for 5 minutes. Add the chicken and garam masala, cover, and simmer gently for 20 minutes, or until the chicken is cooked through and tender. Serve immediately with freshly cooked rice and yogurt.

# chicken cacciatore

## ingredients

### serves 4

3 tbsp olive oil
4 lb/1.8 kg skinless chicken parts
red onions, sliced
2 garlic cloves, finely chopped
14 oz/400 g canned chopped
     tomatoes
2 tbsp chopped fresh flat-leaf
     parsley
1 tbsp sun-dried tomato paste
5 fl oz/150 ml/²/₃ cup red wine
6 fresh basil leaves
salt and pepper
fresh basil sprigs, to garnish
pasta, to serve

## method

1 Heat the olive oil in a flameproof casserole. Add
   the chicken and cook over medium heat, stirring
   frequently, for 5–10 minutes, or until golden. Transfer
   to a plate with a slotted spoon.

2 Add the onions and garlic to the casserole and cook
   over low heat, stirring occasionally, for 10 minutes, or
   until golden. Add the tomatoes, the parsley, tomato
   paste, and wine, and tear in the basil leaves. Season
   to taste with salt and pepper.

3 Bring the mixture to a boil, then return the chicken to
   the casserole, pushing it down into the cooking liquid.
   Cover and cook in a preheated oven, 325°F/160°C, for
   1 hour, or until the chicken is cooked through and
   tender. Garnish with fresh basil sprigs and serve
   immediately with pasta.

# steamed chicken with chile & cilantro butter

## ingredients

*serves 4*

4 tbsp butter, softened
1 fresh Thai chile, seeded
    and chopped
3 tbsp chopped fresh cilantro
4 skinless, boneless chicken
    breasts, about
    6 oz/175 g each
14 fl oz/400 ml/1¾ cups
    coconut milk
12 fl oz/350 ml/1½ cups
    chicken stock
1 cup basmati rice

### pickled vegetables

1 carrot
½ cucumber
3 scallions
2 tbsp rice vinegar
salt and pepper

## method

1 Mix the butter with the chile and cilantro. Cut a deep slash into the side of each chicken breast to form a pocket. Spoon quarter of the flavoured butter into each pocket and place on a 12-inch/30-cm square of baking parchment.

2 Season to taste with salt and pepper, then bring together 2 opposite sides of the paper on top, folding over to seal firmly. Twist the ends to seal. Pour the coconut milk and stock into a large pan with a steamer top. Bring to a boil.

3 Stir in the rice with a pinch of salt. Put the chicken parcels in the steamer top, cover, and simmer for 15–18 minutes, stirring the rice once, until the rice is tender and the chicken is cooked through. Meanwhile, peel the carrot, then trim the carrot, cucumber, and scallions and cut them into fine sticks. Sprinkle with the vinegar.

4 Unwrap the chicken, reserving the juices, and cut in half diagonally. Serve the chicken on the rice, with the juices spooned over and pickled vegetables on the side.

# baked tapenade chicken

## ingredients

*serves 4*

4 skinless, boneless chicken breasts
4 tbsp green olive tapenade
8 thin slices smoked pancetta
2 garlic cloves, coarsely chopped
9 oz/250 g cherry tomatoes,
 halved
4 fl oz/125 ml/scant ½ cup
 dry white wine
2 tbsp olive oil
8 slices ciabatta
salt and pepper

## method

1 Put the chicken breasts on a cutting board and cut three deep slashes into each. Spread a tablespoon of the tapenade over each chicken breast, pushing it into the slashes with a palette knife.

2 Wrap each chicken breast in two slices of pancetta. Place the chicken breasts in a shallow ovenproof dish and arrange the garlic and tomatoes around them. Season to taste with salt and pepper, then pour over the wine and 1 tablespoon of the oil.

3 Bake in a preheated oven, 425°F/220°C, for about 20 minutes, until the juices run clear when the chicken is pierced with a skewer. Cover the dish loosely with aluminum foil and let stand for 5 minutes. Meanwhile, preheat the broiler to high.

4 Brush the ciabatta with the remaining oil and cook under the preheated broiler for 2–3 minutes, turning once, until golden.

5 Transfer the chicken and tomatoes to serving plates and spoon over the juices. Serve the dish with the toasted ciabatta.

# pistachio chicken korma

## ingredients

*serves 4*

1 lb 9 oz/700 g skinless, boneless
chicken breasts or thighs, cut
into 1-inch/2.5-cm cubes
1 tsp salt, or to taste
juice of ½ lemon
4 tbsp ghee or unsalted butter
6 green cardamom pods
1 large onion, finely chopped
2 tsp garlic paste
2 tsp ginger paste
1 tbsp ground coriander
½ tsp chili powder
10 oz/280 g/1¼ cups plain
yogurt, whisked
good pinch of saffron threads,
pounded and soaked in
2 tbsp hot milk
4 oz/115 g/¾ cup shelled
pistachios, soaked in 7 fl oz/
200 ml/scant 1 cup boiling
water for 20 minutes
5 fl oz/150 ml/⅔ cup light cream
2 tbsp rose water
6–8 white rose petals, to garnish
cooked basmati rice and lemon
wedges, to serve

## method

1 Put the chicken in a nonmetallic bowl and add the salt, pepper, and lemon juice. Rub into the chicken, cover, and let marinate in the refrigerator for 30 minutes.

2 Melt the ghee in a medium heavy-bottom saucepan over low heat and add the cardamom pods. When they have puffed up, add the onion and increase the heat to medium. Cook, stirring frequently, until the onion is a pale golden color. Add the garlic paste and ginger paste and cook, stirring frequently, for an additional 2–3 minutes. Add the coriander and chili powder and cook, stirring, for 30 seconds. Add the chicken, increase the heat to medium–high, and cook, stirring continuously, for 5–6 minutes, until it changes color.

3 Reduce the heat to low and add the yogurt and the saffron-and-milk mixture. Bring to a slow simmer, cover, and cook for 15 minutes. Stir halfway through to ensure that it does not stick to the bottom of the pan.

4 Meanwhile, put the pistachios and their soaking water in a blender or food processor and process until smooth. Add to the chicken mixture, followed by the cream. Cover and simmer, stirring occasionally, for an additional 15–20 minutes. Stir in the rose water and remove from the heat. Garnish with the rose petals and serve with cooked basmati rice and lemon wedges.

# chicken with walnut sauce

## ingredients

*serves 4*

4–8 skinless chicken parts
½ lemon, cut into wedges
3 tbsp olive oil
5 fl oz/150 ml/²⁄₃ cup dry
    white wine
10 fl oz/300 ml/1¼ cups
    chicken stock
1 bay leaf
3½ oz/100 g/¼ cup walnut pieces
2 garlic cloves
5 fl oz/150 ml/²⁄₃ cup strained
    plain yogurt
salt and pepper
chopped fresh flat-leaf parsley,
    to garnish
rice or pilaf and pita bread,
    to serve

## method

1 Rub the chicken parts with the lemon. Heat the oil in a large skillet, add the chicken pieces, and fry quickly until lightly browned on all sides.

2 Pour the wine into the skillet and bring to a boil. Add the stock, bay leaf, salt, and pepper and simmer for about 20 minutes, turning several times, until the chicken is tender.

3 Meanwhile, put the walnuts and garlic in a food processor and blend to form a fairly smooth purée.

4 When the chicken is cooked, transfer to a warmed serving dish and keep warm. Stir the walnut mixture and yogurt into the pan juices and heat gently for about 5 minutes until the sauce is quite thick. (Do not boil or the sauce will curdle.) Season with salt and pepper.

5 Pour the walnut sauce over the chicken pieces and serve hot with rice, or pilaf, and pita bread. Garnish with chopped fresh parsley.

# chicken kiev

## ingredients

### serves 4

4 tbsp butter, softened

1 garlic clove, finely chopped

1 tbsp finely chopped fresh parsley

1 tbsp finely chopped fresh
    oregano

4 skinless, boneless chicken breasts

3 oz/85 g fresh white or
    whole wheat bread crumbs

3 tbsp freshly grated Parmesan
    cheese

1 egg, beaten

9 fl oz/250 ml vegetable oil,
    for deep-frying

salt and pepper

slices of lemon and flat-leaf parsley
    sprigs, to garnish

freshly cooked new potatoes and
    selection of cooked vegetables,
    to serve

## method

1 Place the butter and garlic in a bowl and mix together
   well. Stir in the chopped herbs and season well with
   salt and pepper. Pound the chicken breasts to flatten
   them to an even thickness, then place a tablespoon
   of herb butter in the center of each one. Fold in the
   sides to enclose the butter, then secure with wooden
   toothpicks.

2 Combine the bread crumbs and grated Parmesan on
   a plate. Dip the chicken parcels into the beaten egg,
   then coat in the bread crumb mixture. Transfer to a
   plate, cover, and let chill for 30 minutes. Remove from
   the refrigerator and coat in the egg and then the
   breadcrumb mixture for a second time.

3 Pour the oil into a deep-fryer to a depth that will cover
   the chicken parcels. Heat until it reaches 350–375°F/
   180–190°C, or until a cube of bread browns in
   30 seconds. Transfer the chicken to the hot oil and
   deep-fry for 5 minutes, or until cooked through. Lift
   out the chicken and drain on paper towels.

4 Divide the chicken among 4 serving plates, garnish
   with lemon slices and parsley sprigs, and serve with
   new potatoes and a selection of vegetables.

# chicken fricassée

## ingredients

### serves 4

1 tbsp all-purpose flour
salt and white pepper
4 skinless, boneless chicken
    breasts, about 5 oz/140 g each,
    trimmed of all visible fat and
    cut into ¾-inch/2-cm cubes
1 tbsp sunflower or corn oil
8 pearl onions
2 garlic cloves, crushed
8 fl oz/250 ml/1 cup chicken stock
2 carrots, diced
2 celery stalks, diced
8 oz/225 g/2 cups frozen peas
1 yellow bell pepper, seeded
    and diced
4 oz/115 g white mushrooms,
    sliced
4 fl oz/125 ml/½ cup lowfat plain
    yogurt
3 tbsp chopped fresh parsley

## method

1 Spread out the flour on a dish and season with salt and
   pepper. Add the chicken and, using your hands, coat in
   the flour. Heat the oil in a heavy-bottom pan. Add the
   onions and garlic and cook over low heat, stirring
   occasionally, for 5 minutes. Add the chicken and cook,
   stirring, for 10 minutes, or until just beginning to color.

2 Gradually stir in the stock, then add the carrots, celery,
   and peas. Bring to a boil, then reduce the heat, cover,
   and let simmer for 5 minutes. Add the bell pepper and
   mushrooms, cover, and let simmer for an additional
   10 minutes.

3 Stir in the yogurt and chopped parsley and season
   with salt and pepper. Cook for 1–2 minutes, or until
   heated through, then transfer to 4 large, warmed
   serving plates and serve immediately.

# noodles
# & pasta

# noodle basket with chicken-lime salad

## ingredients

*serves 4*

peanut or corn oil, for
　deep-frying and oiling
9 oz/250 g fresh thin or medium
　Chinese egg noodles

**chicken-lime salad**
6 tbsp mayonnaise
6 tbsp sour cream
1-inch/2.5-cm piece fresh ginger,
　peeled and grated
grated rind and juice of 1 lime
4 skinless, boneless chicken thighs,
　poached and cooled, then cut
　into thin strips
1 carrot, peeled and grated
1 cucumber, cut in half lengthwise,
　seeded and sliced
1 tbsp finely chopped fresh cilantro
1 tbsp finely chopped fresh mint
1 tbsp finely chopped fresh parsley
several fresh basil leaves, torn
salt and pepper

## method

*1* To shape noodle baskets, you will need a special set of 2 long-handled wire baskets that clip inside each other, available from gourmet kitchen stores. Dip the larger wire basket in oil, then line it completely and evenly with one-fourth of the tangled noodles. Dip the smaller wire basket in oil, then position it inside the larger basket and clip it into position.

*2* Heat 4 inches/10 cm of oil in a wok or deep-fat fryer to 350–375°F/180–190°C, or until a cube of bread browns in 30 seconds. Lower the baskets into the oil and deep-fry for 2–3 minutes, or until the noodles are golden brown. Remove the baskets from the oil and drain on paper towels. Unclip the 2 wire baskets and carefully remove the small one. Use a round-bladed knife, if necessary, to prise the noodle basket from the wire frame. Repeat to make 3 more baskets. Let the noodle baskets cool.

*3* To make the salad, combine the mayonnaise, sour cream, ginger, and lime rind. Gradually add the lime juice until you get the flavor you like. Stir in the chicken, carrot, cucumber, salt, and pepper. Cover and let chill. Just before serving, stir in the herbs and spoon the salad into the noodle baskets.

# yaki soba

## ingredients

*serves 2*

14 oz/400 g ramen noodles
1 onion, finely sliced
7 oz/200 g fresh bean sprouts
1 red bell pepper, seeded and
    thinly sliced
1 boneless, skin-on cooked
    chicken breast, about
    5½ oz/150 g, sliced
12 cooked, shelled shrimp
1 tbsp peanut oil
2 tbsp shoyu (Japanese soy sauce)
½ tbsp mirin
1 tsp sesame oil
1 tsp toasted sesame seeds
2 scallions, finely sliced

## method

1 Cook the noodles according to the package
  instructions. Drain well and tip into a bowl.

2 Mix the onion, bean sprouts, bell pepper, chicken,
  and shrimp together in a separate bowl. Stir through
  the noodles.

3 Heat a wok over a high heat, then add the peanut oil.
  Add the noodle mixture and stir-fry for 4 minutes, or
  until golden, then add the shoyu, mirin, and sesame oil
  and toss together.

4 Divide the mixture between 2 plates, sprinkle with the
  sesame seeds and scallions, and serve immediately.

# teriyaki chicken with sesame noodles

## ingredients

*serves 4*

4 boneless chicken breasts, about
    6 oz/175 g each, with or
    without skin, as you wish
about 4 tbsp bottled teriyaki sauce
peanut or corn oil
cucumber fans, to garnish

### sesame noodles

9 oz/250 g dried thin buckwheat
    noodles
1 tbsp toasted sesame oil
2 tbsp toasted sesame seeds
2 tbsp finely chopped fresh parsley
salt and pepper

## method

1 Using a sharp knife, score each chicken breast
diagonally across 3 times and rub all over with teriyaki
sauce. Set aside to marinate for at least 10 minutes.

2 When you are ready to cook the chicken, preheat
the broiler to high. Bring a pan of water to a boil, add
the buckwheat noodles, and boil for 3 minutes, or
according to the package instructions, until soft. Drain
and rinse well in cold water to stop the cooking and
remove excess starch, then drain again.

3 Lightly brush the broiler rack with oil. Add the chicken
breasts, skin-side up, and brush again with a little extra
teriyaki sauce. Broil the chicken breasts about 4 inches/
10 cm from the heat, brushing occasionally with extra
teriyaki sauce, for 15 minutes, or until cooked through
and the juices run clear.

4 Meanwhile, heat a wok or large skillet over high heat.
Add the sesame oil and heat until it shimmers. Add the
noodles and stir around to heat through, then stir in
the sesame seeds and parsley. Season with salt and
pepper. To serve, transfer the chicken breasts to plates
and add a portion of noodles to each. Garnish with
cucumber fans.

# chicken chow mein

## ingredients

*serves 4*

9 oz/250 g packet medium
    egg noodles
2 tbsp sunflower oil
10 oz/280 g cooked chicken
    breasts, shredded
1 garlic clove, finely chopped
1 red bell pepper, seeded
    and thinly sliced
3½ oz/100 g shiitake
    mushrooms, sliced
6 scallions, sliced
3½ oz/100 g bean sprouts
3 tbsp soy sauce
1 tbsp sesame oil

## method

1 Place the egg noodles in a large bowl or dish and break
   them up slightly. Pour enough boiling water over the
   noodles to cover and let stand while preparing the
   other ingredients.

2 Preheat a wok over medium heat. Add the sunflower
   oil and swirl it around to coat the sides of the wok.
   When the oil is hot, add the shredded chicken, garlic,
   bell pepper, mushrooms, scallions, and bean sprouts
   to the wok and stir-fry for about 5 minutes.

3 Drain the noodles thoroughly then add them to the
   wok, toss well, and stir-fry for an additional 5 minutes.
   Drizzle the soy sauce and sesame oil over the chow
   mein and toss until well combined.

4 Transfer the chicken chow mein to warmed serving
   bowls and serve immediately.

## variation

Add 1 teaspoon of Chinese five spice to the pan just
before you add the chicken and stir for a few seconds to
release the aromas.

# chicken & green vegetables

## ingredients

### serves 4

9 oz/250 g dried medium Chinese
    egg noodles
2 tbsp peanut or corn oil
1 large garlic clove, crushed
1 fresh green chile, seeded
    and sliced
1 tbsp Chinese five-spice powder
2 skinless, boneless chicken
    breasts, cut into thin strips
2 green bell peppers, cored,
    seeded, and sliced
4 oz/115 g broccoli, cut into
    small florets
2 oz/55 g green beans, trimmed
    and cut into
    1½-inch/4-cm pieces
5 tbsp vegetable or chicken stock
2 tbsp bottled oyster sauce
2 tbsp soy sauce
1 tbsp rice wine or dry sherry
2 oz/55 g/²⁄₃ cup bean sprouts

## method

1 Cook the noodles in a pan of boiling water for
    4 minutes, or according to the package instructions,
    until soft. Drain, rinse, and drain again, then set aside.

2 Heat a wok or large skillet over high heat. Add
    1 tablespoon of the oil and heat until it shimmers.
    Add the garlic, chile, and five-spice powder and stir-fry
    for about 30 seconds.

3 Add the chicken and stir-fry for 3 minutes, or until it is
    cooked through. Use a slotted spoon to remove the
    chicken from the wok and set aside.

4 Add the remaining oil to the wok and heat until it
    shimmers. Add the bell peppers, broccoli, and beans
    and stir-fry for about 2 minutes. Stir in the stock, oyster
    sauce, soy sauce, and rice wine and return the chicken
    to the wok. Continue stir-frying for about 1 minute,
    until the chicken is reheated and the vegetables are
    tender, but still firm to the bite. Add the noodles
    and bean sprouts and use 2 forks to mix all the
    ingredients together.

# pappardelle with chicken & porcini

### ingredients

#### serves 4

1½ oz/40 g dried porcini
    mushrooms
6 fl oz/175 ml/¾ cup hot water
1 lb 12 oz/800 g canned
    chopped tomatoes
1 fresh red chile, seeded and
    finely chopped
3 tbsp olive oil
12 oz/350 g skinless, boneless
    chicken, cut into thin strips
2 garlic cloves, finely chopped
12 oz/350 g dried pappardelle
salt and pepper
2 tbsp chopped fresh flat-leaf
    parsley, to garnish

### method

1 Place the porcini in a small bowl, add the hot water, and let soak for 30 minutes. Meanwhile, place the tomatoes and their can juices in a heavy-bottom pan and break them up with a wooden spoon, then stir in the chile. Bring to a boil, then reduce the heat and let simmer, stirring occasionally, for 30 minutes.

2 Remove the mushrooms with a slotted spoon, reserving the liquid. Strain the liquid into the tomatoes through a coffee filter paper, or a strainer lined with cheesecloth, and let simmer for 15 minutes.

3 Meanwhile, heat 2 tablespoons of the olive oil in a heavy-bottom skillet. Add the chicken and cook, stirring frequently, until golden brown all over and tender. Stir in the mushrooms and garlic and cook for an additional 5 minutes.

4 While the chicken is cooking, bring a large, heavy-bottom pan of lightly salted water to a boil. Add the pasta, return to a boil, and cook for 8–10 minutes, or until tender but still firm to the bite. Drain well, then transfer to a warmed serving dish. Drizzle with the remaining olive oil and toss lightly. Stir the chicken mixture into the tomato sauce, season, and spoon onto the pasta. Toss lightly, sprinkle with parsley, and serve at once.

# spaghetti with parsley chicken

## ingredients

*serves 4*

1 tbsp olive oil

thinly pared rind of 1 lemon,
    cut into julienne strips

1 tsp finely chopped fresh ginger

1 tsp sugar

salt

8 fl oz/250 ml/1 cup chicken stock

9 oz/250 g dried spaghetti

4 tbsp butter

8 oz/225 g skinless, boneless
    chicken breasts, diced

1 red onion, finely chopped

leaves from 2 bunches of
    flat-leaf parsley

## method

*1* Heat the olive oil in a heavy-bottom pan. Add the lemon rind and cook over low heat, stirring frequently, for 5 minutes. Stir in the ginger and sugar, season with salt, and cook, stirring constantly, for an additional 2 minutes. Pour in the chicken stock, bring to a boil, then cook for 5 minutes, or until the liquid has reduced by half.

*2* Meanwhile, bring a large heavy-bottom pan of lightly salted water to a boil. Add the pasta, return to a boil, and cook for 8–10 minutes, or until tender but still firm to the bite.

*3* Meanwhile, melt half the butter in a skillet. Add the chicken and onion and cook, stirring frequently, for 5 minutes, or until the chicken is light brown all over. Stir in the lemon and ginger mixture and cook for 1 minute. Stir in the parsley leaves and cook, stirring constantly, for an additional 3 minutes.

*4* Drain the pasta and transfer to a warmed serving dish, then add the remaining butter and toss well. Add the chicken sauce, toss again, and serve.

# pasta with chicken & feta

## ingredients

### serves 4

2 tbsp olive oil
1 lb/450 g skinless, boneless
    chicken breasts, cut into
    thin strips
6 scallions, chopped
8 oz/225 g Feta cheese, diced
4 tbsp chopped fresh chives
1 lb/450 g dried garganelli
salt and pepper
tomato focaccia, to serve

## method

1 Heat the olive oil in a heavy-bottom skillet. Add the chicken and cook over medium heat, stirring frequently, for 5–8 minutes, or until golden all over and cooked through. Add the scallions and cook for 2 minutes. Stir the Feta cheese into the skillet with half the chives and season with salt and pepper.

2 Meanwhile, bring a large heavy-bottom pan of lightly salted water to a boil. Add the pasta, return to a boil, and cook for 8–10 minutes, or until tender but still firm to the bite. Drain well, then transfer to a warmed serving dish.

3 Spoon the chicken mixture onto the pasta, toss lightly, and serve immediately, garnished with the remaining chives and accompanied by tomato focaccia.

# chicken with creamy penne

## ingredients

### serves 2

7 oz/200 g dried penne
1 tbsp olive oil
2 skinless, boneless chicken
    breasts
4 tbsp dry white wine
4 oz/115 g/¾ cup frozen peas
5 tbsp heavy cream
salt
4–5 tbsp chopped fresh
    parsley, to garnish

## method

1 Bring a large saucepan of lightly salted water to a boil.
   Add the pasta, bring back to a boil, and cook for about
   8–10 minutes, or according to the package directions,
   until tender but still firm to the bite.

2 Meanwhile, heat the oil in a skillet, add the chicken,
   and cook over medium heat for about 4 minutes on
   each side.

3 Pour in the wine and cook over high heat until it has
   almost evaporated. Drain the pasta. Add the peas,
   cream, and pasta to the skillet and stir well. Cover
   and simmer for 2 minutes. Garnish with fresh parsley
   and serve.

# chicken with linguine & artichokes

## ingredients

### serves 4

4 skinless, boneless chicken breasts
finely grated rind and juice of
    1 lemon
2 tbsp olive oil
2 garlic cloves, crushed
14 oz/400 g canned artichoke
    hearts, drained and sliced
9 oz/250 g baby plum tomatoes
10½ oz/300 g dried linguine
chopped fresh parsley and finely
    grated Parmesan cheese,
    to garnish

## method

1 Put each chicken breast in turn between 2 pieces of plastic wrap and bash with a rolling pin to flatten. Put the chicken into a shallow, nonmetallic dish with the lemon rind and juice and 1 tablespoon of the oil and turn to coat in the marinade. Cover and let marinate in the refrigerator for 30 minutes.

2 Heat the remaining oil in a skillet over low heat, add the garlic, and cook for 1 minute, stirring frequently. Add the artichokes and tomatoes and cook for 5 minutes, stirring occasionally. Add about half the marinade from the chicken and cook over medium heat for an additional 5 minutes.

3 Preheat the broiler to high. Remove the chicken from the remaining marinade and arrange on the broiler pan. Cook the chicken under the preheated broiler for 5 minutes each side until thoroughly cooked through. Meanwhile, add the linguine to a pan of boiling water and cook for 7–9 minutes, or until just tender.

4 Drain the pasta and return to the pan, pour over the artichoke and tomato mixture, and slice in the cooked chicken. Divide among 4 warmed plates and sprinkle over the parsley and cheese.

# chicken lasagna

## ingredients

*serves 6*

2 tbsp olive oil
2 lb/900 g/4 cups fresh
　　ground chicken
1 garlic clove, finely chopped
4 carrots, chopped
4 leeks, sliced
16 fl oz/500 ml/2 cups
　　chicken stock
2 tbsp tomato paste
4 oz/115 g Cheddar cheese, grated
1 tsp Dijon mustard
béchamel sauce (see below)
4 oz/115 g dried lasagna
salt and pepper

**béchamel sauce**
20 fl oz/625 ml/2½ cups milk
1 bay leaf
6 black peppercorns
2 slices of onion
mace blade
4 tbsp butter
6 tbsp all-purpose flour
salt and pepper
wild arugula and Parmesan
　　shavings, to serve

## method

*1* To make the béchamel sauce, pour the milk into a pan and add the bay leaf, peppercorns, onion, and mace. Heat gently to just below boiling point, then remove from the heat, cover, let infuse for 10 minutes, then strain. Melt the butter in a separate pan. Sprinkle in the flour and cook over low heat, stirring continuously, for 1 minute. Gradually stir in the milk, then bring to a boil and cook, stirring, until thickened and smooth. Season.

*2* Heat the oil in a heavy-bottom pan. Add the chicken and cook over medium heat, breaking it up with a wooden spoon, for 5 minutes, or until browned all over. Add the garlic, carrots, and leeks, and cook, stirring occasionally, for 5 minutes.

*3* Stir in the chicken stock and tomato paste and season with salt and pepper. Bring to a boil, reduce the heat, cover, and let simmer for 30 minutes.

*4* Whisk half the Cheddar cheese and the mustard into the hot béchamel sauce. In a large ovenproof dish, make alternate layers of the chicken mixture, lasagna, and cheese sauce, ending with a layer of cheese sauce. Sprinkle with the remaining Cheddar cheese and bake in a preheated oven, 375°F/190°C, for 1 hour, or until golden brown and bubbling. Serve immediately, with arugula and Parmesan shavings.

# chicken & wild mushroom cannelloni

## ingredients

*serves 4*

2 tbsp olive oil
2 garlic cloves, crushed
1 large onion, finely chopped
8 oz/225 g wild mushrooms, sliced
12 oz/350 g ground chicken
4 oz/115 g prosciutto, diced
5 fl oz/150 ml/²/₃ cup Marsala wine
7 oz/200 g canned chopped
    tomatoes
1 tbsp shredded fresh basil leaves
2 tbsp tomato paste
10–12 dried cannelloni tubes
butter, for greasing
20 fl oz/625 ml/2½ cups béchamel
    sauce (see page 170)
3 oz/85 g/³/₄ cup freshly grated
    Parmesan cheese
salt and pepper

## method

1 Heat the olive oil in a heavy-bottom skillet. Add the garlic, onion, and mushrooms and cook over low heat, stirring frequently, for 8–10 minutes. Add the ground chicken and prosciutto and cook, stirring frequently, for 12 minutes, or until browned all over. Stir in the Marsala, tomatoes and their can juices, basil, and tomato paste and cook for 4 minutes. Season with salt and pepper, then cover and let simmer for 30 minutes. Uncover, stir, and let simmer for 15 minutes.

2 Meanwhile, bring a large, heavy-bottom pan of lightly salted water to a boil. Add the pasta, return to a boil, and cook for 8–10 minutes, or until tender but still firm to the bite. Using a slotted spoon, transfer the pasta to a plate and pat dry with paper towels.

3 Using a teaspoon, fill the cannelloni tubes with the chicken, prosciutto, and mushroom mixture. Transfer them to a large, lightly greased ovenproof dish. Pour the béchamel sauce over them to cover completely and sprinkle with the grated Parmesan cheese.

4 Bake the cannelloni in a preheated oven, 375°F/190°C, for 30 minutes, or until golden brown and bubbling. Serve immediately.

rice

# chicken fried rice

## ingredients

### serves 4

½ tbsp sesame oil
6 shallots, peeled and cut
    into quarters
3 cups cubed cooked chicken
3 tbsp soy sauce
2 carrots, diced
1 celery stalk, diced
1 red bell pepper, seeded and diced
6 oz/175 g/1¼ cups fresh peas
3½ oz/100 g/⅔ cup drained
    canned corn kernels
9¾ oz/275 g/1¼ cups cooked
    long-grain rice
2 large eggs

## method

**1** Heat a wok or large skillet over a medium heat, add the oil, and heat it.

**2** Add the shallots and fry until soft, then add the chicken and 2 tablespoons of the soy sauce and stir-fry for 5–6 minutes.

**3** Stir in the carrots, celery, red bell pepper, peas, and corn and stir-fry for an additional 5 minutes. Add the rice and stir thoroughly. Beat the eggs and pour into the mixture. Stir until the eggs are beginning to set, then add in the remaining soy sauce. Transfer to bowls and serve immediately.

# risotto with chargrilled chicken breast

## ingredients

*serves 4*

4 boneless chicken breasts, about 4 oz/115 g each

grated rind and juice of 1 lemon

5 tbsp olive oil

1 garlic clove, crushed

8 fresh thyme sprigs, finely chopped

3 tbsp butter

1 small onion, finely chopped

10 oz/280 g/1½ cups risotto rice

5 fl oz/150 ml/²/₃ cup dry white wine

32 fl oz/1 liter/4 cups simmering chicken stock

3 oz/85 g/¾ cup freshly grated Parmesan or Grana Padano cheese

salt and pepper

lemon wedges and fresh thyme sprigs, to garnish

## method

1 Place the chicken breasts in a shallow, nonmetallic dish and season. Mix together the lemon rind and juice, 4 tablespoons of the olive oil, the garlic, and thyme. Spoon over the chicken and rub in. Cover and marinate for 4–6 hours, then return to room temperature.

2 Preheat a grill pan over high heat. Cook the chicken, skin-side down, for 10 minutes, or until the skin is crisp and starting to brown. Turn over and brown the underside. Reduce the heat and cook for 10–15 minutes, or until the juices run clear. Let rest on a carving board for 5 minutes, then cut into thick slices.

3 Meanwhile, melt 2 tablespoons of the butter with the remaining oil in a pan over medium heat. Cook the onion, stirring occasionally, until soft and starting to turn golden. Reduce the heat, stir in the rice, and cook, stirring, for 2–3 minutes, until translucent. Add the wine and cook, stirring, for 1 minute until reduced. Add the hot stock, a ladleful at a time, stirring constantly, until all the liquid is absorbed and the rice is creamy. Season with salt and pepper. Remove from the heat and stir in the remaining butter, then melt in the cheese. Serve at once, topped with the chicken slices and garnished with lemon wedges and thyme sprigs.

# chicken, mushroom & cashew nut risotto

## ingredients

*serves 4*

2 oz/55 g butter
1 onion, chopped
9 oz/250 g skinless, boneless
    chicken breasts, diced
12 oz/350 g/1¾ cups
    risotto rice
1 tsp ground turmeric
5 fl oz/150 ml/²/₃ cup white wine
46 fl oz/1.4 liters/generous
    5½ cups simmering
    chicken stock
2¼ oz/75 g cremini mushrooms,
    sliced
1¼ oz/50 g/scant ⅓ cup cashew
    nuts, halved
salt and pepper
wild arugula, fresh Parmesan
    cheese shavings, and fresh
    basil leaves, to garnish

## method

1 Melt the butter in a large pan over medium heat. Add the onion and cook, stirring occasionally, for 5 minutes, or until softened. Add the chicken and cook, stirring frequently, for an additional 5 minutes. Reduce the heat, add the rice, and mix to coat in butter. Cook, stirring constantly, for 2–3 minutes, or until the grains are translucent. Stir in the turmeric, then add the wine. Cook, stirring continuously, for 1 minute until reduced.

2 Gradually add the hot stock, a ladleful at a time. Stir constantly and add more liquid as the rice absorbs each addition. Increase the heat to medium so that the liquid bubbles. Cook for 20 minutes, or until all the liquid is absorbed and the rice is creamy. About 3 minutes before the end of the cooking time, stir in the mushrooms and cashews. Season with salt and pepper.

3 Arrange the arugula leaves on 4 individual serving plates. Remove the risotto from the heat and spoon it over the arugula. Sprinkle over the Parmesan shavings and basil leaves and serve.

# risotto alla milanese

## ingredients

### serves 4

4½ oz/125 g butter
2 lb/900 g skinless, boneless
    chicken breasts, thinly sliced
1 large onion, chopped
1 lb 2 oz/500 g risotto rice
5 fl oz/150 ml white wine
1 tsp crushed saffron threads
20 fl oz/625 ml/2½ cups
    simmering chicken stock
salt and pepper
fresh flat-leaf parsley sprigs,
    to garnish
2 oz/55 g Parmesan cheese
    shavings, to serve

## method

1 Melt 2 oz/55 g of the butter in a deep skillet. Add the
    chicken and onion and cook over medium heat, stirring
    occasionally, for 8–10 minutes, until golden brown.

2 Reduce the heat, add the rice and cook, stirring
    constantly, for a few minutes until the grains begin
    to swell and are thoroughly coated in the butter.

3 Add the wine and saffron and season with salt and
    pepper. Cook, stirring continuously, until the wine has
    completely evaporated. Add 2 ladlefuls of the hot
    stock and cook, stirring continuously, until it has been
    completely absorbed. Add the remaining stock,
    1 ladleful at a time, stirring continuously and allowing
    each ladleful to be absorbed before adding the next,
    until all the stock has been absorbed and the rice has
    a creamy texture—this will take 20–25 minutes.

4 Garnish each individual plate with a parsley sprig,
    then serve the risotto immediately, sprinkled with
    the Parmesan cheese shavings and dotted with the
    remaining butter.

# chicken basquaise

## ingredients

*serves 4–5*

3 lb/1.3 kg chicken, cut into
    8 parts
flour, for coating
3 tbsp olive oil
1 Bermuda onion, thickly sliced
2 red, green, or yellow bell
    peppers, seeded and cut
    lengthwise into thick strips
2 garlic cloves
5 oz/150 g chorizo sausage,
    skinned and cut into ¹/₂-inch/
    1-cm pieces
1 tbsp tomato paste
7 oz/200 g/1 cup long-grain
    white rice
16 fl oz/450 ml/2 cups chicken
    stock
1 tsp crushed dried chiles
¹/₂ tsp dried thyme
4 oz/115 g Bayonne or other
    air-dried ham, diced
12 dry-cured black olives
2 tbsp chopped fresh parsley
salt and pepper

## method

1 Pat the chicken parts dry with paper towels. Put
   2 tablespoons of flour in a plastic bag, season well
   with salt and pepper, and add the chicken parts.
   Seal the bag and shake to coat the chicken. Heat
   2 tablespoons of the oil in a large flameproof casserole
   over medium–high heat. Add the chicken and cook,
   turning frequently, for 15 minutes, or until well
   browned all over. Transfer to a plate.

2 Heat the remaining oil in the casserole and add the
   onion and bell peppers. Reduce the heat to medium
   and stir-fry until beginning to color and soften. Add the
   garlic, chorizo, and tomato paste and cook, stirring
   continuously, for about 3 minutes. Add the rice and
   cook, stirring to coat, for 2 minutes, or until the rice is
   translucent. Add the stock, crushed chiles, and thyme,
   season to taste with salt and pepper, and stir well.

3 Bring to a boil. Return the chicken to the casserole,
   pressing it gently into the rice. Cover and cook over
   a very low heat for 45 minutes, or until the chicken is
   cooked through and the rice is tender. Stir the ham,
   black olives, and half the parsley into the rice mixture.

4 Re-cover and heat through for another 5 minutes.
   Sprinkle with the remaining parsley and serve the
   casserole immediately.

# chicken & shrimp paella

## ingredients

### serves 6–8

½ tsp saffron threads

2 tbsp hot water

about 6 tbsp olive oil

6–8 chicken thighs, (on the bone, skin on), excess fat removed

5 oz/140 g Spanish chorizo sausage, casing removed, cut into ¼-inch/5-mm slices

2 large onions, chopped

4 large garlic cloves, crushed

1 tsp mild or hot Spanish paprika

13 oz/375 g/generous 1½ cups medium-grain paella rice

3½ oz/100 g green beans, chopped

3 oz/85 g/¾ cup frozen peas

40 fl oz/1.25 liters/5 cups chicken stock

16 live mussels, scrubbed and debearded (discard any that do not shut when tapped)

16 raw shrimp, shelled, and deveined

2 red bell peppers, broiled, peeled, seeded, and sliced

salt and pepper

1¼ oz/35 g fresh parsley, chopped, to garnish

## method

1 Put the saffron threads and water in a small bowl and let infuse for a few minutes.

2 Heat 3 tablespoons of the oil in a 12-inch/30-cm paella pan. Cook the chicken thighs over medium-high heat, turning frequently, for 5 minutes, or until golden and crispy. Transfer to a bowl. Add the chorizo to the pan and cook, stirring, for 1 minute, or until beginning to crisp. Add to the chicken.

3 Heat another 3 tablespoons of the oil in the pan and cook the onions, stirring frequently, for 2 minutes, then add the garlic and paprika and cook, stirring, for 3 minutes, or until the onions are soft, but not browned. Add the rice, beans, and peas and stir until coated in oil. Return the chicken, chorizo, and any juices to the pan. Stir in the stock and the saffron with its soaking liquid, and season with salt and pepper. Bring to a boil, stirring continuously, then let simmer, uncovered, for 15 minutes, or until the rice is almost tender and most of the liquid has been absorbed.

4 Arrange the mussels, shrimp, and red bell pepper slices on top, then cover and let simmer, without stirring, for 5 minutes, or until the shrimp turn pink and the mussels open. Discard any mussels that remain closed. Serve immediately, sprinkled with the parsley.

# sunshine paella

## ingredients

### serves 4–6

½ tsp saffron threads

2 tbsp hot water

5½ oz/150 g cod, rinsed

46 fl oz/1.4 liters/5½ cups
    simmering fish stock

12 large raw shrimp, shelled
    and deveined

7 oz/200 g live mussels,
    scrubbed and debearded

3 tbsp olive oil

5½ oz/150 g chicken breast,
    cut into bite-size chunks

1 large red onion, chopped

2 garlic cloves, chopped

½ tsp cayenne pepper

½ tsp paprika

8 oz/225 g tomatoes, peeled
    and cut into wedges

1 red bell pepper and 1 yellow bell
    pepper, seeded and sliced

12 oz/350 g/1½ cups paella rice

salt and pepper

6 oz/175 g/scant 1 cup canned
    corn kernels, drained

3 hard-cooked eggs, cut into
    fourths lengthwise, to serve

lemon wedges, to serve

## method

1 Put the saffron threads and water in a bowl and let infuse. Cook the cod in the simmering stock for 5 minutes. Rinse, drain, cut into chunks, and set aside in a bowl. Cook the shrimp in the stock for 2 minutes. Add to the cod. Discard any mussels with broken shells or that refuse to close when tapped. Add to the stock and cook until opened. Add to the bowl with the other seafood, discarding any that remain closed.

2 Heat the oil in a paella pan over medium heat. Cook the chicken, stirring, for 5 minutes. Add the onion and cook, stirring, until softened. Add the garlic, cayenne pepper, paprika, and saffron and its soaking liquid and cook, stirring, for 1 minute. Add the tomatoes and bell peppers and cook, stirring, for 2 minutes.

3 Add the rice and cook, stirring, for 1 minute. Add most of the stock, bring to a boil, then let simmer, uncovered, for 10 minutes. Do not stir during cooking, but shake the pan once or twice and when adding ingredients. Season, then cook for 10 minutes, or until the rice is almost cooked, adding more stock if necessary. Add the seafood and corn and cook for 3 minutes.

4 When all the liquid has been absorbed, remove from the heat. Cover and let stand for 5 minutes. Serve topped with egg fourths and garnished with lemon wedges.

# chicken & duck paella with orange

## ingredients

*serves 4–6*

½ tsp saffron threads
2 tbsp hot water
6 oz/175 g skinless, boneless
    chicken breast
4 large skinless, boneless
    duck breasts
2 tbsp olive oil
1 large onion, chopped
2 garlic cloves, crushed
1 tsp paprika
8 oz/225 g tomato wedges
1 orange bell pepper, broiled,
    peeled, seeded and chopped
6 oz/175 g canned red kidney
    beans (drained weight)
12 oz/350 g/1½ cups paella rice
1 tbsp chopped fresh flat-leaf
    parsley, plus extra sprigs
    to garnish
1 tbsp freshly grated orange rind
2 tbsp orange juice
3½ fl oz/100 ml/generous
    ⅓ cup white wine
40 fl oz/1.25 liters/5 cups
    simmering chicken stock
salt and pepper
orange wedges, to garnish

## method

1 Put the saffron threads and water in a small bowl and let infuse for a few minutes.

2 Cut the chicken and duck into bite-size chunks and season. Heat the oil in a paella pan and cook the chicken and duck over medium-high heat, stirring, until golden all over. Transfer to a bowl and set aside.

3 Add the onion and cook over medium heat, stirring, until softened. Add the garlic, paprika, and saffron and its soaking liquid and cook, stirring continuously, for 1 minute. Add the tomato wedges, orange bell pepper, and beans and cook, stirring, for an additional 2 minutes.

4 Add the rice and parsley and cook, stirring, for 1 minute. Add the orange rind and juice, the wine, and most of the hot stock. Bring to a boil, then let simmer, uncovered, for 10 minutes. Do not stir during cooking, but shake the pan once or twice, and when adding ingredients. Return the chicken and duck to the pan and season. Cook for 10–15 minutes, or until the rice grains are plump and cooked, adding a little more stock if necessary.

5 When all the liquid has been absorbed and you detect a faint toasty aroma coming from the rice, remove from the heat. Cover with foil and let stand for 5 minutes. Garnish with parsley sprigs and orange wedges to serve.

# paella with pork & chorizo

## ingredients

*serves 4–6*

12 large raw shrimp, in their shells
2 pints/1.25 liters/5 cups
    simmering fish stock
½ tsp saffron threads
2 tbsp hot water
3½ oz/100 g skinless, boneless
    chicken breast, cut into
    ½-inch/1-cm pieces
3½ oz/100 g pork tenderloin,
    cut into ½-inch/1-cm pieces
3 tbsp olive oil
3½ oz/100 g Spanish chorizo
    sausage, casing removed,
    cut into ½-inch/1-cm slices
1 large red onion, chopped
2 garlic cloves, crushed
½ tsp cayenne pepper
½ tsp paprika
1 red bell pepper, seeded
    and sliced
1 green bell pepper, seeded
    and sliced
12 cherry tomatoes, halved
12 oz/350 g/1½ cups paella rice
1 tbsp chopped fresh parsley
2 tsp chopped fresh tarragon
salt and pepper

## method

1 Add the shrimp to the simmering stock and cook for
2 minutes, then transfer to a bowl and set aside. Put the
saffron threads and water in a small bowl and let infuse.

2 Season the chicken and pork with salt and pepper.
Heat the oil in a paella pan and cook the chicken, pork,
and chorizo over medium heat, stirring, until golden.
Add the onion and cook, stirring, until softened. Add
the garlic, cayenne pepper, paprika, and saffron and
its soaking liquid and cook, stirring continuously, for
1 minute. Add the bell pepper slices and tomato halves
and cook, stirring, for an additional 2 minutes.

3 Add the rice and herbs and cook, stirring continuously,
for 1 minute. Pour in most of the hot stock, bring to a
boil, then let simmer, uncovered, for 10 minutes. Do
not stir during cooking, but shake the pan once or
twice and when adding ingredients. Season, then cook
for an additional 10 minutes, or until the rice is almost
cooked, adding a little more hot stock if necessary.
Add the shrimp and cook for an additional 2 minutes.

4 When all the liquid has been absorbed and you
detect a faint toasty aroma coming from the rice,
remove from the heat. Cover with foil and let stand
for 5 minutes. Serve.

# greek chicken with rice

## ingredients

*serves 4*

8 chicken thighs
2 tbsp corn oil
1 onion, chopped
2 garlic cloves, finely chopped
6 oz/175 g/scant 1 cup
    long-grain rice
7 fl oz/225 ml/scant 1 cup
    chicken stock
1 lb 12 oz/800 g canned
    chopped tomatoes
1 tbsp chopped fresh thyme
2 tbsp chopped fresh oregano
12 black olives, pitted and chopped
2 oz/55 g Feta cheese, crumbled
fresh oregano sprigs, to garnish

## method

1 Remove the skin from the chicken. Heat the oil in
   a flameproof casserole. Add the chicken, in batches,
   if necessary, and cook over medium heat, turning
   occasionally, for 8–10 minutes, or until golden. Transfer
   to a plate with a perforated spoon.

2 Add the onion, garlic, long-grain rice, and 2 fl oz/50 ml/
   scant ¼ cup of the stock to the casserole and cook,
   stirring, for 5 minutes, or until the onion is softened.
   Pour in the remaining stock and add the tomatoes and
   their juices and the herbs.

3 Return the chicken thighs to the casserole, pushing
   them down into the rice. Bring to a boil, then reduce
   the heat, cover, and simmer for 25–30 minutes, or
   until the chicken is cooked through and tender. Stir in
   the olives and sprinkle the cheese on top. Garnish with
   oregano sprigs and serve immediately.

# jambalaya

## ingredients

### serves 4

14 oz/400 g skinless, boneless
    chicken breast, diced
1 red onion, diced
1 garlic clove, crushed
20 fl oz/625 ml/2½ cups
    chicken stock
14 oz/400 g canned chopped
    tomatoes in tomato juice
10 oz/280 g/generous 1½ cups
    brown rice
1–2 tsp hot chili powder
½ tsp paprika
1 tsp dried oregano
1 red bell pepper, seeded
    and diced
1 yellow bell pepper, seeded
    and diced
3 oz/85 g/½ cup frozen corn kernels
3 oz/85 g/½ cup frozen peas
3 tbsp chopped fresh parsley
pepper
crisp salad greens, to serve

## method

1 Put the chicken, onion, garlic, stock, tomatoes, and rice into a large, heavy-bottom pan. Add the chili powder, paprika, and oregano and stir well. Bring to a boil, then reduce the heat, cover, and let simmer for 25 minutes.

2 Add the red and yellow bell peppers, corn, and peas to the rice mixture and return to a boil. Reduce the heat, cover, and let simmer for an additional 10 minutes, or until the rice is just tender (brown rice retains a 'nutty' texture when cooked) and most of the stock has been absorbed but is not completely dry.

3 Stir in 2 tablespoons of the parsley and season with pepper. Transfer the jambalaya to a warmed serving dish, garnish with the remaining parsley, and serve with crisp salad greens.

# egg-fried rice with chicken

## ingredients

*serves 4*

8 oz/225 g/generous 1 cup
  jasmine rice
3 skinless, boneless chicken
  breasts, cut into cubes
14 fl oz/400 ml/1¾ cups canned
  coconut milk
1¼ oz/50 g block creamed
  coconut, chopped
2–3 cilantro roots, chopped
thinly pared zest of 1 lemon
1 fresh green chile, seeded
  and chopped
3 fresh Thai basil leaves
1 tbsp fish sauce
1 tbsp oil
3 eggs, beaten
fresh chives and sprigs fresh
  cilantro, to garnish

## method

1 Cook the rice in boiling water for 12–15 minutes, drain
  well, then let cool and chill overnight.

2 Put the chicken into a pan and cover with the coconut
  milk. Add the creamed coconut, cilantro roots, lemon
  zest, and chile, and bring to a boil. Let simmer for 8–10
  minutes, until the chicken is tender. Remove from the
  heat. Stir in the basil and fish sauce.

3 Meanwhile, heat the oil in a wok and stir-fry the rice
  for 2–3 minutes. Pour in the eggs and stir until they
  have cooked and mixed with the rice. Line 4 small
  ovenproof bowls or ramekins with plastic wrap and
  pack with the rice. Turn out carefully onto serving
  plates and remove the plastic wrap. Garnish with long
  chives and sprigs of cilantro. Serve with the chicken.

# hainan chicken rice

## ingredients

*serves 4–6*

1 chicken, weighing
   3 lb 5 oz/1.5 kg
2 oz/55 g fresh young ginger,
   smashed
2 garlic cloves, smashed
1 scallion, tied in a knot
1 tsp salt
2 tbsp vegetable or peanut oil
chili or soy dipping sauce,
   to serve

### rice

2 tbsp vegetable or peanut oil
5 garlic cloves, finely chopped
5 shallots, finely chopped
12 oz/350 g/scant 1¾ cups
   long-grain rice
30 fl oz/940 ml/3¾ cups
   chicken stock
1 tsp salt

## method

1 Wash the chicken and dry thoroughly. Stuff the body cavity with the ginger, garlic, scallion, and salt.

2 In a large pan, bring enough water to a boil to submerge the chicken. Place the chicken in the pan, breast-side down. Bring the water back to a boil, then turn down the heat and simmer, covered, for 30–40 minutes. Turn the chicken over once.

3 Remove the chicken and wash in running cold water for 2 minutes to stop the cooking. Drain, then rub the oil into the skin. Set aside.

4 To prepare the rice, heat the oil in a preheated wok or deep pan. Stir-fry the garlic and shallots until fragrant. Add the rice and cook for 3 minutes, stirring rapidly. Transfer to a large pan and add the chicken stock and salt. Bring to a boil, then turn down the heat and let simmer, covered, for 20 minutes. Turn off the heat and let steam for an additional 5–10 minutes, or until the rice is perfectly cooked.

5 To serve, chop the chicken horizontally through the bone and skin into chunky wedges. Serve with the rice and a chili or soy dipping sauce.

# chicken steamed with rice in lotus leaves

## ingredients

*serves 4–8*

1 lb/450 g/generous 2 cups
  glutinous rice, soaked in cold
  water for 2 hours
16 fl oz/450 ml/1¾ cups cold water
1 tsp salt
1 tsp vegetable or peanut oil
4 dried lotus leaves, soaked in
  hot water for 1 hour

### filling

3½ oz/100 g raw small shrimp,
  shelled and deveined
2-inch/5-cm piece fresh ginger
7 oz/200 g lean chicken meat,
  cut into bite-size strips
2 tsp light soy sauce
2 oz/55 g dried Chinese
  mushrooms, soaked in warm
  water for 20 minutes
1 tbsp vegetable or peanut oil
7 oz/200 g cha siu or pork loin
1 tbsp Shaoxing rice wine
1 tsp dark soy sauce
½ tsp white pepper
1 tsp sugar

## method

*1* For the filling, steam the shrimp for 5 minutes and set aside. Finely grate the ginger, discarding the fibrous parts on the grater and reserving the liquid that drips through. Marinate the chicken in the light soy sauce and ginger juices for at least 20 minutes. Steam for a few minutes in the marinade. Set aside.

*2* Drain the rice and place in a pan with the water. Bring to a boil, then add the salt and oil. Cover and cook over very low heat for 15 minutes. Divide into 8 portions and set aside. Squeeze out any excess water from the mushrooms, then finely slice, discarding any tough stems. Reserve the soaking water. In a preheated wok or deep pan, heat the oil and stir-fry the pork, shrimp, and mushrooms for 2 minutes. Stir in the Shaoxing, dark soy sauce, pepper, and sugar. Add the reserved mushroom soaking water, if necessary.

*3* Rinse and dry the lotus leaves. Place a portion of rice in the center of each and flatten out to form a 4-inch/10-cm square. Top with the pork mixture and some pieces of chicken. Top with another portion of rice, then fold the lotus leaf to form a tight package. Steam for about 15 minutes. Let rest for 5 minutes, then serve.

# chicken with vegetables & cilantro rice

## ingredients

### serves 4

2 tbsp vegetable or peanut oil
1 red onion, chopped
2 garlic cloves, chopped
1-inch/2.5-cm piece fresh ginger, peeled and chopped
2 skinless, boneless chicken breasts, cut into strips
4 oz/115 g white mushrooms
14 oz/400 g canned coconut milk
2 oz/50 g sugar snap peas, trimmed and halved lengthwise
2 tbsp soy sauce
1 tbsp fish sauce

### rice

1 tbsp vegetable or peanut oil
1 red onion, sliced
12 oz/350 g/3 cups rice, cooked and cooled
8 oz/250 g bok choy, torn into large pieces
handful of fresh cilantro, chopped
2 tbsp Thai soy sauce

## method

1 Heat the oil in a wok or large skillet and sauté the onion, garlic, and ginger together for 1–2 minutes.

2 Add the chicken and mushrooms and cook over high heat until browned. Add the coconut milk, sugar snap peas, and sauces, and bring to a boil. Let simmer gently for 4–5 minutes until tender.

3 Heat the oil for the rice in a separate wok or large skillet and cook the onion until softened, but not browned. Add the cooked rice, bok choy, and fresh cilantro, and heat gently until the leaves have wilted and the rice is hot. Sprinkle over the soy sauce and serve immediately with the chicken.

# chicken biryani

## ingredients

### serves 8

1½ tsp finely chopped fresh ginger

1½ tsp crushed fresh garlic

1 tbsp garam masala

1 tsp chili powder

½ tsp ground turmeric

2 tsp salt

5 green/white cardamom
    pods, crushed

10 fl oz/300 ml/1¼ cups
    plain yogurt

3 lb 5 oz/1.5 kg chicken, skinned
    and cut into 8 parts

5 fl oz/150 ml/⅔ cup milk

1 tsp saffron strands

6 tbsp ghee

2 onions, sliced

1 lb/450 g basmati rice

2 cinnamon sticks

4 black peppercorns

1 tsp black cumin seeds

4 fresh green chiles

4 tbsp lemon juice

2–3 tbsp finely chopped fresh
    cilantro leaves

## method

1 Blend the ginger, garlic, garam masala, chili powder, turmeric, half the salt, and the cardamoms together in a bowl. Add the yogurt and chicken parts and mix well. Cover and let marinate in the refrigerator for 3 hours.

2 Boil the milk in a small pan, pour over the saffron, and set aside.

3 Heat the ghee in a large pan. Add the onions and cook until golden. Transfer half of the onions and ghee to a bowl and set aside.

4 Place the rice, cinnamon sticks, peppercorns, and black cumin seeds in a pan of water. Bring to a boil and remove from the heat when the rice is half-cooked. Drain and place in a bowl. Mix with the remaining salt.

5 Chop the chiles and set aside. Add the chicken mixture to the pan containing the onions. Add half each of the chopped green chiles, lemon juice, cilantro, and saffron milk. Add the rice, then the rest of the ingredients, including the reserved onions and ghee. Cover tightly and cook over low heat for 1 hour. Check that the meat is cooked through; if it is not cooked, return to the heat, and cook for an additional 15 minutes. Mix well before serving.